THE FRENCH REVOLUTION OF 1789: IT'S WAR ON THE CLASSICAL PILLARS OF WESTERN SOCIETY AND THE RISE OF SECULARISM

An In-Depth Analysis of the Revolution's Attack on the Catholic Church, Ancien Régime (Monarchy, Clergy, Nobility), Tradition, Patriarchy, and Primogeniture

By

CHRISTOPHER E. ROSS B.S., MBA, M.S.
SANCTUS VIRTUE PUBLISHING DEARBORN, MICHIGAN

© 2024 Sanctus Virtue Publishing, Dearborn, Michigan

All rights reserved

ISBN: 979-8-9916647-0-7

Library of Congress catalogue and card number: 2024920675

Printed in the United States of America

The French Revolution of 1789: Transcended a mere political upheaval; it represented a deliberate and systematic assault on the foundational pillars of Western civilization. By dismantling the Catholic Church, monarchy, and long-standing traditions, the Revolution became a pivotal catalyst for the rise of secularism and the gradual erosion of the classical moral and social order. While modernism—the synthesis of all heresies, as cautioned by Pope Pius X—did not emerge solely from this event, the Revolution undeniably set the stage for the profound challenges that both the Church and society continue to grapple with today. Its far-reaching implications reverberate throughout modernity, marking a decisive turning point in the trajectory of Western thought and values.

Table of Contents

Introduction 1

Chapter 1:

Interwoven Realms: The Catholic Church, Papacy, Government, and Social Order in Pre-Revolutionary France 8

The King of Pre-Revolutionary France 9

The Aristocracy and the Concept of Privilege in Pre-Revolutionary France.. 11

The Ecclesiastical Order of Pre-Revolutionary France 13

Their Mission and Aims 15

Marriage and Family in Pre-Revolutionary France 15

Patriarchy and Inheritance Laws in Pre-Revolutionary France 17

The Peasants of Pre-Revolutionary France 19

The Church's Monopoly on Religion... 20

Education in Pre-Revolutionary France 23

Chapter 2:

The Rise of Deism: Enlightenment's Rebellion against the Classical Social Order of Kingship, Nobility, Tradition, and the Church 25

Rousseau's Social Contract Theory: Birth of Modern Democracy in the Enlightenment 29

Voltaire.. 31

The Declaration of the Rights of Man and the Citizen 32

Revolutionary Changes to the Family Structure 36

Revolutionary Inheritance Laws: Ending Patria Potestas in France......39

Revolutionary Reforms Concerning the Privileges of the Aristocracy ...42

The Catholic Church and its Role in Pre-Revolutionary France.............44

Chapter 3:

Subjugating Faith: The French Revolution's Overthrow of Catholic Church Authority 46

Breaking Ecclesiastical Power: Secular Education, Hospitals and Poor Relief 51

Secular Rebellion: How Freedom of Conscience Confronted Catholic Hegemony 54

Desecrated Domains: The Nationalization of Church Property& and the Abolition of the Tithe..55

Revolutionary Attacks on Monasticism and the Taking of Vows 58

Before and After: France's Relationship with the Papacy through the Revolution.. 61

The Impact of De-Christianization on Revolutionary France's Religious Landscape 63

Revolutionary Secularization: The Takeover of Parish Registers and Its Impact 64

The Church Besieged: Catholic Clergy and the French Revolution's Terror 66

Redefining Time: How the French Revolution Created a New Calendar 69

Chapter 4:

What Replaced Papal Monarchy, the Aristocracy, Spiritual Oversight of the Catholic Church, and Tradition?.. 71

The Self-Crowned Emperor: Napoleon's Secular Assertion Against the Church 74

Conclusion 76

Bibliography 83

INTRODUCTION

In the tumultuous period preceding the French Revolution, the fabric of French society was intricately woven with the threads of the Catholic Church, the monarchy, and a deeply entrenched aristocratic system. The interplay between these institutions created a complex social order that governed every aspect of life, from the grandeur of the royal court to the humble villages of the peasantry. The king of pre-revolutionary France stood at the apex of this hierarchy, embodying the divine right to rule, while the aristocracy enjoyed privileges reinforcing their dominance. The ecclesiastical order wielded immense spiritual and temporal power, maintaining a monopoly on religion and education and shaping societal norms surrounding marriage, family, marriage, morality, culture, and politics.

As Enlightenment ideas began to permeate society, figures such as Rousseau and Voltaire challenged the classical social order with the rise of deism (the belief that a creator exists but does not intervene in the universe), the denial of original sin and the adoption of John Lock's Tabula Rasa [blank slate] theory, the revolutionaries began advocating for principles of popular sovereignty and individual rights. These revolutionary ideas set the stage for profound changes that would dismantle the classical regime. The Declaration of the Rights of Man and the Citizen[1], for instance, signaled a new era where privileges based on birthright and ecclesiastical power were questioned and ultimately overturned.

This book delves into the transformative impact of the French Revolution on the established social, political, and religious structures of pre-revolutionary France. It examines the revolutionary reforms that redefined family structures, inheritance laws, and the privileges of the aristocracy. Furthermore, it explores the secularization efforts that subjugated religious authority, nationalized church property, and promoted freedom of conscience. By scrutinizing the radical shifts in the relationship between the state and the Church and the reconfiguration of societal norms, this chapter provides a comprehensive understanding of how revolutionary ideals reshaped France's historical trajectory.

This book argues that the French Revolution fundamentally disrupted the interwoven realms of the Catholic Church, the monarchy, and the aristocracy by introducing secular, democratic principles that redefined the social order. Through a series of revolutionary reforms, the revolution dismantled the traditional structures of privilege, ecclesiastical power, and patriarchal norms. This led to are configuration of French society that emphasized individual rights, secular governance, and equality before the law.

"The Revolution treated the Church much as it treated the monarchy. Sovereignty in the person of the Pope was inverted. ***The Church was subordinated to the nation***; Pope Pius VI was eliminated – first burned in effigy in 1791, then actually imprisoned in France, where he died in Valence in 1799. Clerics were chosen by and made responsible to the electorate created by the Revolution."[1]

To properly understand how profound it was to make the Catholic Church and the papacy subordinated to the secular state of France, it would be best to look at the classical role and foundations of the Catholic Church, a good place to look at the nature of spiritual and temporal power, or in other words church and state power and the proper relationship thereof, is to look at some of the text of the Unam Sanctum which was a papal bull issued by Pope Boniface VIII in 1302:

"...Hence we must recognize the more clearly that spiritual power surpasses in dignity and in nobility any temporal power whatever, as spiritual things surpass the temporal... Therefore, if the terrestrial power err, it will be judged by the spiritual power;

---

[1] Kennedy, Emmet. *A Cultural History of the French Revolution*. New Haven, Yale University Press, 1989.

but if a minor spiritual power err, it will be judged by a superior spiritual power; but if the highest power of all err, it can be judged only by God, and not by man... Furthermore, we declare, we proclaim, we define that it is absolutely necessary for salvation that every human creature be subject to the Roman Pontiff."[2]

Through this papal bull, we see the classical function of the Catholic Church and the papacy and that there are two powers on Earth: the spiritual power and the temporal power. The Catholic Church and the papacy represent spiritual power because they care for the human soul, while temporal power represents the power over the physical body and earth, which belongs to the king and/or secular authorities. The role of the spiritual power was to guide the secular power, meaning, for example, if a church official made a judgment in a civil or criminal case, the state secular officials would carry out that judgment, using force if need be. If, for example, a cleric deemed an offender a heretic and sentenced him or her to exile, it was the duty of the temporal authority to carry out that exile by force if need be.

However, the predominant theme of the Catholic Church in its classical function was to be the spiritual oversight of government. This means that if a secular/temporal power errs somehow, the spiritual authority would be able to provide a check and balance upon it to bring it back into proper moral functionality. For example, if a secular ruler acted against the interests of the Church and/or acted against the spiritual interest of the faithful, it could issue an edict of excommunication against that ruler, which would free his subjects from obedience to him.

Because power corrupts, because men are sinful, they are in need of spiritual oversight. As we know, the old saying goes, "Power corrupts, yet absolute power corrupts absolutely." We know from the Petrine Doctrine that the Church Jesus Christ set upon the rock of St. Peter is the Catholic Church, that the gates of Hades shall not prevail against it, and that the Holy Spirit guides

---

[2] Internet History Sourcebooks Project. Sourcebooks.fordham.edu, sourcebooks.fordham.edu/source/B8-unam.asp.

the Church until the end of time. Because Jesus said the gates of Hades should not overcome the Church and the Holy Spirit guides the Catholic Church, it provides a proper spiritual oversight over secular authorities. When the Catholic Church was in its proper function, it provided the moral basis of society as we know it.

There were numerous benefits for society when the Pope, bishops, and Church were the spiritual oversight of temporal authorities. One of the main benefits was political, Eiusdemreligionis idem imperium (religious unity begets political unity, also "one religion, one empire," "same religion, same rule"). When people of a society share the same religion, it is a source of political unity, and it promotes harmony within society as well as cooperation between its members. In contrast to today's multicultural and multi-religious societies, there is actually very little unity and cooperation between its members politically. Religion does matter because what a person believes religiously has much to do with their values, and what determines their values also determines their actions and how they see the world.

According to Huntington (1993), "First, the differences among civilizations are not only real; they are basic. Civilizations are differentiated from each other by history, language, culture, tradition, and, most important, religion. The people of different civilizations have different views on relations between God and man, the individual and the group, the citizen and the state, parents and children, husband and wife, as well as differing views on the relative importance of rights and responsibilities, liberty and authority, equality and hierarchy. These differences are the product of centuries. They will not soon disappear."[3] When the West was all Catholic, which it was for centuries, the West was properly labeled Christendom. This brought unity, and because the Pope was the main oversight of Christendom, it provided a sense of common identity and shared moral values between people and territories of Christendom; it brought a sense of harmony between Christians.

---

[3] Huntington, S. P. (1993). The clash of civilizations? Foreign Affairs, 72(3), 25

When there was papal oversight over temporal rulers, it provided a moral compass for rulers and people and ensured that Christian values and ethics were the moral basis of political rule. When there was spiritual oversight, the laws passed were made to promote justice and charity and protect the weak and vulnerable. It worked to provide ethical government and a check and balance on political power and political rulers because Popes and bishops were direct advisors of kings and emperors.

This spiritual oversight and advisory worked to curb absolute power from excesses and promoted ethical governance. With spiritual oversight, the Church controlled the facets of education, which preserved the knowledge of orthodoxy and/or sound doctrine, which brought about unity on sound doctrine, and protected the kingdoms and people from heresy, which means things that go against sound doctrine and divide Christians into schismatic sects.

There was also less conflict between nations and kingdoms because the Pope would act as the arbitrator between powers, and because each nation shares the same religious beliefs, often peace would come faster when the Pope mediated the conflict between two warring nations. When there was spiritual oversight of temporal rulers, temporal rulers enjoyed lasting security of their rule because the ruler got his legitimacy from the Church, and this would enable the ruler to rule as God's representative on Earth because it would work to protect the interests of the Church and faithful, which gave temporal rulers lasting legitimacy in the eyes of their subjects.

Spiritual oversight provided numerous benefits: proper moral education was instilled in the people and rulers, the spiritual welfare of society was looked after, and spiritual oversight provided social cohesion between people. It was the source of spiritual integration within society and aimed to create a society based on true Christian principles, true morality, and true godliness.

As stated, the result of the French Revolution was taking the Church out of the function of being above the state and making it subordinate to the state, reversing the natural order, and making the state the oversight of the Church, which is what turned our world upside down as we know it, and what gave the final push for complete secularization of society; which gave birth to the modern age as we know it today.

Based on my studies, if we want to reawaken the true spirit of Christianity in society today, we must undo what the French Revolution officials did and reassert the Church to its proper place again, being the spiritual oversight of temporal power once again. The missing key to bringing godliness and morality back into society again is to place the Catholic Church where the classical world placed it, to give it back control over matters concerning spiritual interests and bring it back to being the spiritual oversight of temporal authority, meaning the Church is the gatekeeper of morality, not secular authorities.

During the French Revolution, the unseating of the Church was gradual; it did not all happen at once but occurred through a series of steps. In this chapter, we will explore the major steps secular governmental officials took to make this happen. We will also delve into the classical world before the Revolution to provide readers with a clear picture of how church-state relations operated in both classical and medieval times and how the French Revolution and its actors took steps to subordinate the Church to the state.

We will examine privilege and hierarchy, the influence of the philosophical concept of deism on revolutionaries, the transition of schools from being Catholic to secular, the assumption of poor relief duty by revolutionaries, the abolition of the tithe and its effects, the declaration of rights which contradicted the powers of the Church to combat heresy, and more.

Additionally, we will study how the secular state took over family law, marriage, and divorce, changed inheritance laws, undermined the authority of fathers, promoted religious tolerance at the expense of combating heresy, shifted focus away from death and final judgment to material happiness, disempowered the clergy, granted rights to Jews and heretics, implemented universal manhood suffrage and popular sovereignty, treated heretics and believers equally, and disempowered the Church by seizing its wealth and land.

The dechristianization campaign of the French Revolution will be thoroughly examined, along with how the state took control of the parish register, changed the calendar, abolished church censorship, and influenced society through Enlightenment ideals. We will discuss how constitutionalism altered government operations and examine the attack on clerical celibacy.

Furthermore, we will analyze how churches were transformed into secular monuments, religious holidays were replaced with secular ones, and secular symbols replaced religious ones, as well as the impact of these changes on society. We will explore the effect of nationalizing church lands, the abolition of monastic vows, the assault on patriarchy, the true nature of conservatism and liberalism, and the discussion of democracy versus divine right. Finally, we will discuss divine providence, the rise of Napoleon, and in the final chapter the potential steps future leaders can take to restore the Catholic Church to its proper role as the spiritual overseer of society once again.

CHAPTER 1:

INTERWOVEN REALMS: THE CATHOLIC CHURCH, PAPACY, GOVERNMENT, AND SOCIAL ORDER IN PRE-REVOLUTIONARY FRANCE

In pre-revolutionary France, the concept of divine providence held significant sway over both religious and secular affairs, serving as a fundamental belief that God actively governed the universe and intervened in human affairs for the greater good. Rooted in Christian theology, divine providence was perceived as the guiding force behind historical events, shaping the destiny of nations and individuals according to God's will. The view of divine providence is that Catholicism is the source of social cohesion and morality, that the world is governed by divine providence, and that the world is not solely governed by human action, innovation, reason, and progress, as many deists and Enlightenment thinkers think today.[4] The Catholic Church, as the spiritual authority, played a central role in promulgating this belief, emphasizing God's sovereignty and benevolence in all aspects of life.

The Pope, as the highest spiritual authority within the Church, was seen as God's representative on Earth and wielded considerable influence in matters of divine providence. Through papal pronouncements and decrees, the Pope affirmed the divine right of kings, asserting that monarchs ruled by God's grace and were accountable to Him alone. This belief conferred legitimacy upon the monarchy and reinforced the hierarchical structure of society, with the king and nobility viewing themselves as divinely appointed rulers tasked with upholding God's order on Earth. By aligning themselves with divine providence, the Catholic Church

---

[4] Desan, S., & Company, T. (2013). Living the French Revolution and the Age of Napoleon. The Great Courses, pg. 226

and the Pope exercised significant control over the king and nobility, shaping their actions and decisions in accordance with religious principles and ensuring the maintenance of social stability and order.

In-pre-revolutionary France, the social and government order was based on hierarchy:

"In the Old Regime—French society before 1789—hierarchy structured every relationship: the king over his subjects, lords over their peasants, men over women, masters over slaves in the colonies, and clergy over laypeople. At the time, even those on the bottom of this structure believed that hierarchy was natural—sanctioned by God."[5]

THE KING OF PRE-REVOLUTIONARY FRANCE

In pre-revolutionary France, the king operated as the supreme ruler, guided by the political ideology of the divine right of kings, which asserted that his authority to govern was granted directly by God. This belief not only legitimized his rule but also placed him above all earthly authorities. The king's primary tasks included maintaining national security, administering justice, overseeing foreign affairs, and ensuring the prosperity of the kingdom. He collected revenue through various taxes, including the taille, gabelle, and aides, as well as feudal dues from the nobility.

The king was both revered and obeyed by his subjects, viewed as God's representative on Earth. He had the power to pass laws, which were often issued as royal decrees, and he convened and dissolved the Estates-General at his discretion. The Catholic Church and the Pope sanctioned his rule, providing spiritual endorsement and reinforcing the belief in his divine right. This alliance between the monarchy and the Church further solidified the king's absolute authority and helped maintain the societal hierarchy of the classical order.

---

[5] Ibid.

The king used the philosophy of Divine Right to rule the kingdom. The belief was that the king was not subject to any earthly authority, only accountable to God, and that he exercised supreme power on Earth[6]:

> "It is in my person alone that sovereign power resides...It is from me alone that my courts derive their authority; and the plenitude of this authority, which they exercise only in my name, remains always in me...It is to me alone that legislative power belongs, without any dependence and without any division... The whole public order emanates from me, and the right and interests of the nation...are necessarily joined with mine and the rest only in my hands."[7]

The kings' duties were to uphold the supremacy of the Church and its doctrine, to rid the kingdom of heretics, to prevent disorder in society, to make sure justice was upheld, and to forever maintain the "prerogative of the Order of the Holy Spirit," and that no duelist would be pardoned under his reign.[8] In the classical world, their power was not absolute because the Pope held the spiritual authority, the Pope consecrated Kings, and the Pope had the power to excommunicate Kings, which would free his subjects from their oaths of obedience to the excommunicated king. Throughout classical history, the Pope acted as the spiritual oversight of secular leaders.

---

[6] Kennedy, Emmet. A Cultural History of the French Revolution. New Haven, Yale University Press, 1989, pg. 297
[7] Doyle, W. (2018). The Oxford History of the French Revolution. Oxford University Press, pg. 38
[8] Ibid, pg. 1

THE ARISTOCRACY AND THE CONCEPT OF PRIVILEGE IN PRE-REVOLUTIONARY FRANCE

In pre-revolutionary France, the concept of equality before the law as we understand it today did not exist. Society was stratified into different groups with distinct legal statuses based on their function and position. The highest status was held by the nobility or aristocracy and the clergy. Their privilege stemmed from societal roles: the aristocracy were warriors, and the clergy provided spiritual and moral oversight. This division exempted both groups from taxation, as their duties to the state were seen as their contribution. The aristocracy, expected to fight for the nation when necessary, were freed from taxation because their military service was their obligation to the state. Similarly, the clergy, tasked with the spiritual care of the nation, also enjoyed tax exemption. This system placed the tax burden primarily on the peasants, leading to widespread resentment and envy toward the privileged classes. This discontent was one of the driving forces behind the French Revolution.

Aristocrats also had the privilege of collecting seigneurial dues from peasants. These dues, rooted in the feudal system, included various forms of payments and labor that peasants owed to their local lords in exchange for the use of land and protection. Dues like the cens (rent), the champart (a portion of the harvest), and the corvée (unpaid labor) were crucial for maintaining the seigneurs' estates but fueled peasant discontent and social unrest. The aristocracy was a hereditary class where noble titles and privileges were passed down through generations. This system was based on the belief that noble lineage bestowed inherent qualities of leadership, valor, and loyalty, essential for the realm's stability and governance. Nobles were expected to uphold their family's honor through bravery, military service, and fulfilling their social duties. This hereditary commitment fostered deep loyalty to the crown, ensuring governance continuity and stability over centuries. The exemption from taxes and the collection of seigneurial dues reinforced the social and economic hierarchy, perpetuating a stable societal order.

Honor was a central concept within the aristocracy, deeply linked to their identity and social standing. For nobles, honor was a collective family legacy to be maintained and enhanced over generations, encompassing virtues like bravery, loyalty, integrity, and fulfilling social and familial duties. Military service was a primary demonstration of honor, with nobles expected to be skilled warriors and leaders, showcasing their courage and commitment to the crown. Their behavior and etiquette were governed by a strict code of conduct, ensuring dignity, courtesy, and respect in their interactions and responsibilities.

Honor also involves protecting and enhancing the family name. Marriages were arranged to strengthen alliances and bolster family prestige, while actions that could tarnish the family's reputation were avoided. Duels were a common means of defending one's honor against personal slights, illustrating the lengths nobles would go to maintain their social standing. This complex and vital concept reinforced the social hierarchy and norms of pre-revolutionary France, ensuring that nobles remained paragons of virtue, loyalty, and leadership. The nobility held significant social, political, and economic power, serving as military leaders, holding key administrative and judicial positions, and managing vast estates.

Exempting from most taxes due to historical privileges granted by the monarchy in exchange for military service and loyalty, they instead collected rents, dues, and feudal obligations from peasants. The nobility, including dukes, marquises, counts, viscounts, barons, and knights, supported the king and maintained the hierarchical structure of the classical order. Their inherited wealth and status perpetuated their influence and privileges within French society.

Nobles enjoyed numerous privileges and distinctions, such as precedence at public events, exclusive trials, and a unique mode of execution if convicted of capital crimes. They were exempt from duties like the corvée, billeting of troops, and militia conscription and enjoyed fiscal advantages and were free from the taille tax. Engaging in retail trade was dishonorable for nobles, risking demotion to commoner status.[9] The social

---

[9] Doyle, W. (2018). The Oxford History of the French Revolution. Oxford University Press, pg. 27-33

hierarchy reflected the medieval division into those who worked, fought, and prayed, with the clergy ranking above the nobility as the first order of the realm in law.

The privileges of the nobility were a source of deep antagonism and one of the underlying themes of the French Revolution. Revolutionary officials aimed to destroy the hierarchy and privileges to promote egalitarianism. The nobility's different legal status was tied to their military service and continued allegiance to the crown over generations. The Revolution sought to eliminate these distinctions, pushing for a society based on equality rather than hereditary privilege.[10]

THE ECCLESIASTICAL ORDER OF PRE-REVOLUTIONARY FRANCE

The classical world before the French Revolution was often based on the concept of privilege, which was different from the equality and egalitarianism we live in today's society. A person's role and function in society often determine whether they are privileged. Because the Catholic Church and its officials were the spiritual oversight of society, they were guardians of the moral order because they had many functions, such as advising kings, educating people, providing hospital services, providing poor relief services, etc. They had the privilege of not paying taxes and collecting the tithe. In pre-revolutionary France, the tithe (la dîme) was a mandatory tax paid to the Catholic Church, representing about one-tenth of a person's agricultural produce, including grains, wine, fruits, and livestock, with variations depending on the region and type of produce.

Payment of the tithe was organized through local church authorities and collected annually, typically during harvest. The funds collected from the tithe were used to support the local parish clergy, maintain church buildings, and fund various religious activities, thereby playing a crucial role in sustaining the Church's presence and functions within the community. The essence of the Church's privilege was the tax exemption because

---

[10] Desan, S., & Company, T. (2013). Living the French Revolution and the Age of Napoleon. The Great Courses.

society at the time looked at the clergy as those who pray, and those who pray were the gatekeepers of the moral order, which is why they were given tax exemption because it was a godly and noble endeavor.[11]

In pre-revolutionary France, the Pope held a significant role in both religious and political affairs, wielding considerable influence over the Catholic Church's operations within the kingdom. The Pope served as the supreme spiritual leader of the Church, responsible for upholding doctrinal orthodoxy, appointing bishops, and overseeing ecclesiastical matters. One of the Pope's key functions was to collect money from various sources, including tithes and donations, to fund the Church's activities and maintain its infrastructure. These financial resources not only supported the Church's religious missions but also contributed to its political power and influence.

Additionally, the Pope often played a diplomatic role in supporting the king and maintaining stability within the kingdom. Through papal bulls and decrees, the Pope could provide spiritual legitimacy to royal policies and actions, thereby reinforcing the authority of the monarchy. Furthermore, the Pope's support for bishops and other clergy members helped solidify their allegiance to the king, ensuring that the Church remained a supportive ally of the monarchy. Overall, the Pope's role in pre-revolutionary France encompassed a wide range of functions, from spiritual leadership and doctrinal oversight to diplomatic and political support for the monarchy. Through his authority and influence, the Pope played a crucial role in shaping the religious and political landscape of pre-revolutionary France, contributing to the stability and legitimacy of the classical order.

---

[11] Desan, S., & Company, T. (2013). Living the French Revolution and the Age of Napoleon. The Great Courses.

THEIR MISSION AND AIMS

- Served as educators and promoters of religious education, instructing both clergy and laity in matters of faith and doctrine.

- Played a crucial role in maintaining social order and stability by reinforcing moral and ethical standards within the community.

- Acted as mediators and arbitrators in resolving disputes and conflicts among the populace, providing guidance and counsel based on religious principles.

- Administered charity and alms, distributing resources to the impoverished and marginalized members of society.

- Participated in diplomatic efforts, serving as intermediaries between the Church and secular authorities to negotiate treaties and resolve conflicts.

- Conducted religious ceremonies and rites of passage, including baptisms, confirmations, weddings, and funerals, which were integral to the spiritual and social fabric of society.

MARRIAGE AND FAMILY IN PRE-REVOLUTIONARY FRANCE

In pre-revolutionary France, marriage and family were deeply influenced by social, economic, and religious factors, with arranged marriages being common, especially among the nobility. These unions were often orchestrated to preserve and strengthen family alliances, ensure the continuity of noble bloodlines, and consolidate wealth and power. The Catholic Church governed marriage through canon law, viewing it as both a sacrament and a binding contract. This perspective underscored the sacred nature of marriage, making it a spiritual commitment that could not be dissolved by human authority, thus rendering divorce impermissible. The Church reinforced the importance of family stability and societal order by treating marriage as a lifelong bond. This system helped maintain social stability in the kingdom, as the interconnected web of noble families supported the hierarchical structure and fostered loyalty to the crown and the Church.

These marriage alliances often played a crucial role in political strategy, influencing territorial claims, inheritance rights, and diplomatic relations. The careful orchestration of these unions ensured that power remained within established elite circles, further entrenching the nobility's dominance and enduring influence over French society. This intricate network of familial and political connections created a resilient social fabric, which both supported and was supported by the monarchy and the Church, thereby perpetuating the existing social order and providing a measure of stability in a period often marked by conflict and change.

In pre-revolutionary France, church authorities administered canon law to families through a comprehensive system of ecclesiastical oversight. Canon law, established by the Catholic Church, governed various facets of family life, including marriage, legitimacy, and moral conduct. Before marriage, couples underwent a series of steps mandated by canon law, such as public announcements of their intent to marry and pre-marital examinations by priests to ensure their understanding and consent. The wedding ceremony itself had to be conducted by a priest in a church, with the marriage recorded in parish registers. Additionally, the Church maintained meticulous parish records of baptisms, which established the legitimacy of children and their status within the community.

Parish priests provided moral guidance to families, reinforcing Church teachings on family life, sexual behavior, and familial roles. Disputes and issues related to family matters were adjudicated in ecclesiastical courts staffed by clergy knowledgeable in canon law and operating under the authority of the bishop. Enforcement of canon law was ensured through ecclesiastical penalties such as excommunication or interdict, which could be applied to individuals or communities violating church regulations. Overall, the administration of canon law by church authorities formed a pervasive system that governed many aspects of family life, contributing to the maintenance of social order and religious adherence in pre-revolutionary France.

PATRIARCHY AND INHERITANCE LAWS IN PRE-REVOLUTIONARY FRANCE

In pre-revolutionary France, patriarchy was deeply ingrained in societal structures, reflecting the dominance of male authority within families and broader social institutions. Patriarchy existed as a means of maintaining social order and stability, with power and privilege concentrated in the hands of men. This system was closely tied to the hierarchical structure of society, which mirrored the centralized authority of the monarchy. Just as the king held supreme authority over the nation, fathers held authority over their households, reinforcing the notion of paternalistic rule.

The patriarchal system served to uphold the established social order and support the monarchy by aligning familial authority with the overarching authority of the king. It contributed to stability by emphasizing obedience and deference to male figures, ensuring that familial and societal structures remained intact. Patriarchy was also deeply intertwined with the Christian social order, as it reflected biblical teachings on the roles of men and women within the family and society.

In pre-revolutionary France, the concept of "letters de cachet" empowered the head of the household, or patria potestas, with significant authority over his family, including the ability to imprison his children and wives. This legal instrument, a sealed letter signed by the king, allowed a father to request the incarceration of family members without a trial, often to enforce discipline, maintain family honor, or manage unruly behavior. This patriarchal power reinforced strong family governance, ensuring the male head maintained control and authority within the household. By enabling fathers to swiftly address family issues internally, the system reduced the need for external intervention by law enforcement. Consequently, this mechanism contributed to societal stability and order, obviating the necessity for a modern police force by allowing families to govern themselves under the patriarch's strict oversight, thus preserving the hierarchical and moral structure of society.

According to Christian doctrine, men were regarded as the heads of households, responsible for providing for and protecting their families, while women were expected to submit to their husbands' authority and prioritize domestic duties. This alignment with Christian principles reinforced the patriarchal system and justified male dominance within both the family and wider society.

Overall, patriarchy in pre-revolutionary France served as a cornerstone of the social and political order, bolstering the authority of the monarchy, maintaining stability, and aligning with religious beliefs about gender roles and hierarchy.

In pre-revolutionary France, primogeniture was a legal and customary practice where the eldest son inherited the entirety of his parents' estate, particularly among the nobility. This system existed to maintain family wealth, consolidate power, and ensure the continuity of noble lineages. By concentrating land, titles, and resources in the hands of the eldest son, primogeniture prevented the fragmentation of estates and the dilution of familial power. It provided stability by preserving the status quo within noble families, preventing internal conflicts over inheritance, and reducing the risk of territorial disputes.

Primogeniture was closely associated with the monarchy, as it mirrored the centralized authority of the king. Just as the king held sovereignty over the realm, the eldest son held authority over the family's estates, reinforcing the hierarchical structure of society. Additionally, primogeniture reinforced the ties between noble families and the monarchy, as the eldest son often served as a loyal vassal to the king, providing military service and political support in exchange for land grants and titles. This system also maintained the nobility's social standing and prestige, ensuring wealth and titles remained within established noble families. By passing down estates to the eldest son, primogeniture preserved the family's influence and enabled successive generations to maintain their privileged societal position. Overall, primogeniture in pre-revolutionary France played a crucial role in preserving wealth, power, and social order within noble families. It strengthened the connection between nobility and monarchy, provided stability, and reinforced the hierarchical structure of society.

THE PEASANTS OF PRE-REVOLUTIONARY FRANCE

In pre-revolutionary France, peasants comprised the largest segment of society, engaging primarily in agricultural activities on the lands owned by nobles, clergy, and the monarchy. Their daily labor involved tasks such as cultivating crops, caring for livestock, and harvesting produce, all of which were crucial for the kingdom's economic prosperity and food supply. Peasants fulfilled their obligations by paying taxes and dues to their landlords, including contributions to the Church and feudal obligations to the nobility.

Despite their indispensable role in supporting the kingdom's economy, peasants occupied a lower social status with limited autonomy. They were subject to the authority of the nobles, clergy, and monarchy, who held sway over land ownership, legal matters, and governance. Peasants adhered to the demands of their landlords, providing labor and services in exchange for protection and access to land. The peasants, according to the following quotation, were seen as the third estate:

> "A sixteenth-century document explains: The head is the King. The arms are the nobility. The feet are the third estate. The arms must carry food to the mouth...The clergy is the heart. It is swollen with tithes. It will have to give some of them up...Each must be kept in his Estate...The three estates are members of one body of one province which is mother to all of them. One man is seen as equal to another before death and the final judgment, when, of course, no earthly rank will be considered."[12]

---

[12] Kennedy, Emmet. A Cultural History of the French Revolution. New Haven, Yale University Press, 1989, pg. 15

THE CHURCH'S MONOPOLY ON RELIGION

In pre-revolutionary France, the Catholic Church was the sole religious authority based on the Petrine Doctrine, exerting a monopoly on religion deeply entrenched in the established social and cultural order. The Church's influence extended to every aspect of life, with its teachings and practices woven into the fabric of society. It governed key life events such as births, marriages, and deaths, regulating these rites through sacraments and rituals that reinforced its spiritual authority. Deviation from Catholic doctrine was considered heresy, and heretics were dealt with severely through the Inquisition, which aimed to root out and punish dissenting beliefs. Additionally, other religions were generally marginalized and suppressed to maintain the Catholic Church's hegemony.

Religious freedom posed a threat to the established order because it challenged the Church's supremacy and undermined its control over societal norms and values. As a powerful institution, the Church sought to maintain its influence and authority by suppressing dissent and enforcing conformity to its teachings. Any deviation from Catholicism was seen as a threat to social cohesion and stability, as it could potentially weaken the Church's grip on the hearts and minds of the populace. Therefore, the Catholic Church maintained its monopoly on religion to preserve its dominance and ensure conformity to its religious and moral standards, thus reinforcing the hierarchical structure of pre-revolutionary French society.

According to orthodox belief, the Catholic Church is not just another religion in the world; it represents Christ's original church set up upon the rock of St. Peter by Jesus Himself[13], whereby the legitimacy of the Catholic Church was bolstered by its rightful claim of enjoying apostolic unbroken succession, and that bishops are the direct line and successors of the apostles of Jesus Christ through unbroken succession by the laying of hands. This exclusive monopoly on Christianity rests upon the Petrine

---

[13] "And I tell you, you are Peter, and on this rock I will build my church, and the gates of hell shall not prevail against it." (Matthew 16:18, ESV)

Doctrine that Jesus Christ divinely sanctioned the Apostle Peter to build His Church, and the office of St. Peter was passed down to the Pope, as the see of Peter.

The monopoly on the Christian religion was not manmade in this sense; it was divinely ordained, and opposition to a divinely ordained endeavor was often looked at as heresy. The reason why the Catholic Church held a monopoly on religion is that its origins are not manmade but divinely sanctioned by Jesus Christ Himself, and heresies and sects were seen as manmade human innovations that sought to lead humanity astray from sound doctrine into heresy, thus threatening the salvation of souls and promoting societal and individual instability and misguidance. Heretics were looked at as the "wolves in sheep's clothing" because they sought to eternally damn souls through misguidance and to divide Christians against one another into manmade sects.

In pre-revolutionary France, the Catholic Church played a multifaceted role in regulating both spiritual and secular aspects of society. As the official registrar of the nation, the Church maintained records of births, marriages, and deaths, serving as the primary source of vital statistics for the populace. Furthermore, the Church actively enforced religious orthodoxy and moral standards, punishing blasphemy and sacrilege to uphold the sanctity of religion and public morality. Offenders faced a range of legal penalties, including fines, imprisonment, flogging, and even execution, depending on the severity of the offense and deterring others from offending. In addition to its judicial functions, the Church acted as a censor, scrutinizing and censoring any literature deemed detrimental to religion and morals. This control extended to books and pamphlets, with the Church wielding significant authority in determining what could be disseminated to the public.

Moreover, the Church collected tithes, bolstered by state support, if necessary, further solidifying its financial and political influence. As the sole recognized religion, Catholicism monopolized religious practice, with the Church's authority rooted in the Petrine Doctrine, asserting its continuity with Christ's original teachings. Additionally, the Church's vast land holdings endowed it with considerable power and influence over society, reinforcing its position as a central institution in pre-revolutionary French life.

In pre-revolutionary France, the Catholic Church served as a powerful censor tasked with regulating the dissemination of books, pamphlets, and other publications deemed harmful to the faith and morals of the populace. This role was paramount in maintaining the Church's authority and preserving social cohesion within the kingdom. By exercising control over printed materials, the Church aimed to safeguard Catholic doctrine and prevent the spread of ideas that challenged its teachings or undermined religious orthodoxy. Publications deemed heretical, blasphemous, or morally objectionable were subject to censorship, with the Church wielding significant influence over what could be published and disseminated to the public.

This censorship was seen as crucial for upholding the spiritual well-being of society, as it protected individuals from exposure to ideas that could lead them astray from the teachings of the Church and disrupt the established social order. Additionally, by controlling the flow of information, the Church reinforced its role as the ultimate arbiter of truth and morality, ensuring that its authority remained unchallenged and that the faithful remained steadfast in their adherence to Catholic doctrine. Overall, the Church's censorship efforts in pre-revolutionary France played a vital role in safeguarding religious orthodoxy, preserving social stability, and upholding the dominance of Catholicism within French society.

In pre-revolutionary France, the Church had immense political power and an absolute monopoly on public worship. The king, along with all his subjects as far as the law was concerned, were Catholics.[14] Protestants, who were a new heretical, schismatic sect, had no legal toleration and no civil rights, as people did not have the right to practice heresy. The entire educational system was under the control of the Catholic Church, and the majority of hospitals and poor relief were also under the

---

[14] Doyle, W. (2018). The Oxford History of the French Revolution. Oxford University Press, pg. 36

Catholic Church. Its censorship powers were vital to the moral framework of the nation; it guarded people from immorality and heresy, as a shepherd guards his sheep from wolves, and the pulpit was used for important announcements and warnings.[15]

It was a privilege to be able to disseminate written material. To win this privilege, the works could not have anything that would harm government, morals, and religion.[16] When it came to the actual practice of censorship in pre-revolutionary France, it was practiced by the Parliament of Paris, the theological faculty at Sorbonne, and the Paris police, whom the bishops assisted.[17] When a person wanted to publish something, they had to obtain a license and submit their work to the censors before it could be published, and this is why the press never grew as it did in other places.[18]

EDUCATION IN PRE-REVOLUTIONARY FRANCE

In pre-revolutionary France, education was largely under the influence and control of the Catholic Church, reflecting its central role in shaping both religious and secular aspects of society. Education was deeply religious, with Catholic doctrine permeating every aspect of the curriculum. The Church emphasized the importance of education in cultivating moral virtue and religious piety, viewing it as a means of nurturing faithful Christians and upholding the social order.

The curriculum focused heavily on the liberal arts, drawing inspiration from the classical education of ancient times. Subjects such as Latin, rhetoric, philosophy, and theology were prioritized, reflecting the Church's commitment to preserving and transmitting knowledge from antiquity. This education system differed significantly from today's secular model, as religious instruction was integrated into every subject, and the primary goal was the spiritual and moral formation of students.

---

[15] Ibid
[16] Ibid, pg. 6
[17] Kennedy, Emmet. A Cultural History of the French Revolution. New Haven, Yale University Press, 1989, pg. 14
[18] Ibid

Moreover, education in pre-revolutionary France played a crucial role in preparing leaders for the monarchy. The Church's control over education ensured that future rulers received a comprehensive education steeped in Catholic doctrine and monarchist ideals. Nobles and members of the aristocracy were educated in exclusive institutions such as Jesuit schools or royal academies, where they were groomed for leadership roles within the monarchy. This education instilled in them a sense of duty, honor, and loyalty to the crown, reinforcing the hierarchical structure of society and perpetuating the divine right of kings. Overall, education in pre-revolutionary France was deeply intertwined with religion and monarchy, serving as a tool for upholding both spiritual and temporal authority in society.

The classical education endeavors of pre-revolutionary France were heavily rooted in the study of Latin classics, and at least four hours a day was dedicated to the study of Ancient Rome and its culture, which worked to keep people connected to the past, which gave the people a strong cultural bond to the social order. Most of the remaining courses were rooted in ensuring that Catholic orthodoxy was taught, which, in other words, means sound doctrine.[19] Studying the rich literary Latin texts and history of the Latin classics kept people connected to the past, enabling them to relate to its rich history and continue its legacy.

It also reinforced a collective cultural identity, which helped keep the culture strong because it is deeply rooted. Because the Latin classics are amazing models of mastered rhetoric, grammar, and logic, they worked to enhance the students' linguistic and literary capabilities. The classical Latin texts and the study of Roman history worked to encourage critical thinking, logical analysis, and an understanding of great philosophical ideas. The Latin classics inspired the great virtues of civic duty, honor, bravery, and self-sacrifice, and they worked to build the character of the students. This education instilled in the people sound Catholic doctrine and the wisdom of the Latin classics, which enabled them to judge human affairs from a higher perspective.

---

[19] Doyle, W. (2018). The Oxford History of the French Revolution. Oxford University Press, pg. 49

CHAPTER 2:

THE RISE OF DEISM: ENLIGHTENMENT'S REBELLION AGAINST THE CLASSICAL SOCIAL ORDER OF KINGSHIP, NOBILITY, TRADITION, AND THE CHURCH

The Enlightenment, an intellectual movement sweeping Europe in the 17th and 18th centuries, found fertile ground in prerevolutionary France, profoundly transforming the nation's cultural and philosophical landscape. Rooted in reason, empirical evidence, and a challenge to established norms, the Enlightenment championed ideas that directly confronted the foundations of French society, including the monarchy, hierarchy, nobility, tradition, and the Catholic Church. Central to this transformation was the rise of Deism and Theophilanthropy, movements that redefined religious belief. Deism, a rational approach to spirituality, posited a creator who set the universe in motion but did not interfere in human affairs, thus rejecting the Church's dogma and divine intervention.

Theophilanthropy, combining a love of God and humanity, further distanced itself from orthodox Christianity by promoting a simple, moralistic faith rooted in human reason and ethics. These new perspectives were seen as heretical, challenging the divine right of kings, the entrenched social hierarchy, the privileged nobility, and the long-held traditions upheld by the Catholic Church. As Enlightenment thinkers like Voltaire, Rousseau, and Montesquieu critiqued these institutions, they laid the intellectual groundwork for revolutionary changes, chipping away at the old order and paving the way for a society based on equality, secularism, and individual rights.

Based on Enlightenment perspectives and general thought, a man by the name of Jean-Baptiste Chemin-Dupontès came up with a new type of religion to compete with Catholicism that was based on universalist perspectives called theophilanthropy, which in its literal translation means "love of God and man."[20] The foundation of the deist belief was the opposite of that of divine providence, which was the belief that God created the world, set up the laws of nature, and left human beings to their own devices.[21] The code of deism was a simple universal one: "Adore God, love your neighbors, make yourself useful to the nation."[22] The deists turned theophilanthropy into a new religion; instead of clerics, fathers often led their families in worship to this new religion. They even sang hymns, invoked prayers for the nation, read from deistic texts, and even began to take this new religion to the Catholic Churches, and at times got into ritual battles with Catholics and clergy.[23]

These new deists saw themselves as enlightened because they created a universalist religion that could apply to everyone who was not stuck in what they perceived as a "rigid doctrine." They began to denounce priests because they saw Christianity as a religion that simply perpetuated constant civil disorder.[24] This new religion/philosophy of deism took strong root in France during this time, and eventually, this new philosophy was looked at as superior to classical Catholic doctrine. Classical Catholic doctrine was eventually made subordinate to this new philosophy and heresy called deism.

In classical Catholic doctrine, the concept of original sin holds that all humans are born with a sinful nature due to the disobedience of Adam and Eve in the Garden of Eden. This original sin, inherited by all descendants of the first humans, marks everyone from birth with a moral defect that inclines them toward sin and estranges them from God. According to Catholic teaching, this inherent sinfulness necessitates divine grace and

---

[20] Desan, S., & Company, T. (2013). Living the French Revolution and the Age of Napoleon. The Great Courses, 222-223
[21] Ibid
[22] Ibid
[23] Desan, S., & Company, T. (2013). Living the French Revolution and the Age of Napoleon. The Great Courses, 222-223
[24] Ibid

redemption through the sacraments, particularly baptism, which cleanses the soul of this primal stain.

In stark contrast, the Enlightenment philosopher John Locke proposed the idea of tabula rasa, or the blank slate, arguing that each person is born without innate ideas or predispositions. For Locke, the human mind is shaped entirely by experience and education, suggesting that a predetermined sinful nature does not bind individuals but is free to develop their character through personal and societal influences. This fundamental opposition between the Catholic view of original sin and Locke's notion of the blank slate highlights the shift from a theological understanding of human nature to one based on empirical observation and reason, reflective of the broader intellectual transformations of the Enlightenment era.

This new Enlightenment thinking based on the rejection of original sin, meant using criticism, that by using human reason, we can improve, and that we must use human reason to promote human happiness here on Earth, and that we should use our reason and bodies to improve and be useful to humanity as a whole.[25] They began to believe that men could communicate directly with God without any intermediaries, and they started to place heavy emphasis on the "God of nature" instead of Jesus and somehow placed their inspiration for this new religion on the "beauty of nature."[26] Instead of focusing on the salvation of the soul, they started to place heavy emphasis on achieving human happiness on Earth and that a state should be based upon the inclination to achieve happiness on Earth, and to achieve this happiness, they desired to form a new government.[27]

They did not wholly abandon the belief in Jesus Christ; they did wholly abandon the idea of original sin and the need for atonement, and they simply reduced the role of Jesus to a type of Socratic status instead of being the savior of humanity.[28] Instead of emphasizing sound Catholic doctrine as Christendom had

---

[25] Doyle, W. (2018). The Oxford History of the French Revolution. Oxford University Press, pg. 149
[26] McManners, John. The French Revolution and the Church. Church Historical Society, 1969, pg. 77-78
[27] Ibid
[28] Ibid, pg. 14

been for over one thousand years, the need to purify doctrine and root out heresies was traded for Enlightenment thinking with a new sense of tolerance and a call for the brotherhood of all men and that all men are part of humanity.[29]

Instead of relying on sound Catholic doctrine to be the center of the social order and the means to judge the morality of society and humanity, the Enlightenment began to be a blend of 18th-century philosophy and 19th-century positivism and began to use a type of skepticism in religion. They sought an educational system free from religious influences, and reason itself being the basis of morality instead of doctrine, and when it came to human behavior, they sought empirical evidence sparking from the study of biology and other sciences as a way to understand human behavior.[30]

They began to see classical Catholicism as the source of all strife in the world and chose to live according to what they believed to be natural law instead. Many began to reject the idea of an afterlife, that death was simply an eternal sleep, that this life is all we have, and that we might as well make the best of it now. They began to equate morality with reason and interest and that the ideas of self-preservation were paramount in the quest for morality and human happiness; they even began to call this doctrine the "counter catechism."[31]

They sought to move away from monarchy and sound Catholic doctrine and decided to build a society based on what they perceived to be scientific and rational principles.[32] Because many of the revolutionaries did not believe in the salvation of the soul and the sanctification of the soul, they became entirely worldly. They began to base nearly everything on whether it is useful for society to achieve worldly happiness now. Does it appeal to reason, or is it, as they called it, superstitious? They

---

[29] Kennedy, Emmet. A Cultural History of the French Revolution. New Haven, Yale University Press, 1989, pg. 147
[30] Kennedy, Emmet. A Cultural History of the French Revolution. New Haven, Yale University Press, 1989, pg. 59
[31] Ibid
[32] Desan, S., & Company, T. (2013). Living the French Revolution and the Age of Napoleon. The Great Courses, pg. 150

tried to compel the clergy to stop emphasizing the afterlife and compelled them to try to improve life here and now.[33]

ROUSSEAU'S SOCIAL CONTRACT THEORY: BIRTH OF MODERN DEMOCRACY IN THE ENLIGHTENMENT

The Enlightenment, a period marked by the flourishing of ideas centered on reason, individualism, and skepticism of traditional authority, profoundly influenced Jean-Jacques Rousseau and his seminal work, "The Social Contract." Inspired by the intellectual currents of his time, Rousseau envisioned a society where governance is based on the collective will of the people rather than the divine right of kings. His theory posited that legitimate political authority arises from a social contract agreed upon by all citizens, promoting the principles of liberty and equality. This radical notion challenged the entrenched power of monarchies and the divine rights of kings, laying the groundwork for modern democratic thought and chipping away at the foundations of absolute rule. Through "The Social Contract," Rousseau articulated a vision of political legitimacy that resonated deeply with Enlightenment ideals, ultimately contributing to the decline of monarchical power and the rise of democratic governance.

Using Enlightenment ideas, Rosseau argued against the divine right of the king's theory, which meant that sovereignty rested in the king alone; rather, he argued that sovereignty rested in the people who agreed to a type of social contract. He believed that instead of being controlled by a king or a powerful church, society should be governed by the general will of the people, which acts as a collective moral force that would call for the general good of society. This general good would best be communicated and better expressed through laws written by a legislature to be elected by the people.

Since Rousseau believed that sovereignty should rest with the people as a whole, a type of popular sovereignty, since it would be based on the general will of the people, he believed that laws

---
[33] Ibid, pg. 82

would reflect the general will and that general will of the people would be good for the whole.[34] Rousseau used Enlightenment principles to come up with a political philosophy that would create a government system in which people can be equal, free, and moral at the same time.[35] He viewed monarchy as arbitrary because it was not based on the consent of the people; he argued for a type of social contract that instead of surrendering their liberty and sovereignty to a ruler or even representatives, people should surrender it to each other as a collective group.[36]

He argued that the right to rule was based on the people agreeing to this contract, that instead of the people being ruled by an arbitrary ruler, a collective force emanating from the general will would govern society for what he perceived as the general good.[37] He believed that this system would only work if the people were moral and virtuous. Because they are virtuous, this would enable them to recognize the general will and then implement it politically for the good of all.[38] For more detailed information about the social contract theory and the divine right of kings, please be on the lookout for our upcoming book about this subject.

The effect of Rosseau's social contract theory inspired the French Civil Constitution, which read that sovereignty 'rests essentially in the nation.' This radical new view regarding sovereignty made all citizens free and equal in rights with each other; it called for the preservation of rights when it came to liberty, security, property, and resistance to oppression, and it helped shape the political world to stop arbitrary arrest and imprisonments, it brought forth the ethos of a presumption of guilt before judgment, and brought forth equality of the law, and ushered in a new tax system based on a citizens capacity to pay, it called forth for the freedom of speech and communication as a

---

[34] Desan, S., & Company, T. (2013). Living the French Revolution and the Age of Napoleon. The Great Courses, pg. 25
[35] Ibid
[36] Ibid, pg. 23-24
[37] Desan, S., & Company, T. (2013). Living the French Revolution and the Age of Napoleon. The Great Courses, pg. 23-24
[38] Ibid, pg. 24

whole, all these things were a direct attack on the old regimes privilege.[39]

VOLTAIRE

Voltaire, born François-Marie Arouet in 1694, was a quintessential figure of the Enlightenment whose writings and ideas profoundly influenced the intellectual landscape of his time. A prolific writer, he propagated Enlightenment principles such as reason, freedom of thought, and skepticism of authority through his essays, plays, and books. Voltaire was particularly known for his vehement anti-Catholicism, criticizing the Church's dogma and its role in suppressing individual freedoms, most famously through his rallying cry, "Écrasezl'infâme" ("Crush the infamous thing").

His contributions to the development of social contract theory, emphasizing the importance of individual rights and the social contract as a foundation for legitimate governance, also left a lasting impact on political philosophy. Voltaire's advocacy for civil liberties and his critique of autocratic power resonated deeply with the revolutionaries of late 18th-century France, thus playing a crucial role in shaping the ideological underpinnings of the French Revolution.

---

[39] Doyle, W. (2018). The Oxford History of the French Revolution. Oxford University Press, pg. 118

THE DECLARATION OF THE RIGHTS OF MAN AND THE CITIZEN

The Declaration of the Rights of Man and the Citizen, adopted by the National Constituent Assembly of France in August 1789, is a significant document in the history of human rights and democratic governance. Written during the early stages of the French Revolution, it was primarily authored by General Lafayette with contributions from Thomas Jefferson and influenced by Enlightenment thinkers such as Voltaire and Rousseau. The Declaration aimed to articulate the fundamental rights and freedoms inherent to all individuals, providing a foundational text for the emerging French Republic.

The Declaration contains a preamble and 17 articles outlining the natural rights of men, including liberty, property, security, and resistance to oppression. It emphasizes the equality of all citizens before the law, the sovereignty of the people, and the necessity for laws to reflect the general will. This document was crafted during a period of significant change, driven by the desire to reform the feudal structures and absolute monarchy that had been prevalent in French society.

Contrary to the Divine Right of Kings theory, which claimed that monarchs derived their authority from God, the Declaration asserts that political power originates from the people and must be based on their consent. It also challenges the influence of the Catholic Church by advocating for freedom of religion and the separation of church and state. By rejecting the notion of divine sanction for both monarchy and papal oversight, the Declaration contributed to the development of secular governance and individual rights, influencing subsequent democratic movements.

Many influential people during the French Revolution saw the monarchy as a type of despotism. They viewed monarchy as the worst of all governments because subjects of a monarchy often had no rights and little or no security.[40] They sought to set up a parliament along with the Declaration of Rights, and even

---

[40] Doyle, W. (2018). The Oxford History of the French Revolution. Oxford University Press, pg. 59

though they did not see a parliament as perfect, it seemed safer than a monarchy because it offered protection from a "despotic autocrat."[41] Because many people during this time had a strong disdain for monarchy, hierarchy, and aristocratic privilege, they dismantled the system of feudal dues and established the Declaration of the Rights of Man and Citizen to establish equality before the law, as opposed to the once different legal statuses of pre-revolutionary France.[42]

In spite of the censorship the French had to follow, meaning they were not free to publish things contrary to faith and morals, with this new Declaration, they had freedom of speech and the right to publish freely, and they had a right to a fair trial, and that citizens were recognized with a type of universal rights.[43] The French Revolution was not identical to the American Revolution; it had similarities but was different.

The Declaration was about "liberty, property, security, and resistance to oppression."[44] They sought to undue pre-revolutionary France almost entirely, to overturn privilege, meaning to stop what they viewed as an unfair tax system, to stop the king from imprisoning people without a trial, etc. It sought to end privilege and offered everybody equality of opportunity in government. It sought an equal taxation basis, allowed all citizens to participate in law-making, and instead of the king guarding the gates of morality and privilege, it changed the function of government to guard and preserve the rights of the people.[45]

The Declaration of the Rights of Man and Citizen was about universal rights. It was in line with a representative government enacted to protect what they believed to be the inherent rights of the people, and it was driven by popular sovereignty. It worked to cancel out all the inequities of what they called the old system

---

[41] Ibid
[42] Desan, S., & Company, T. (2013). Living the French Revolution and the Age of Napoleon. The Great Courses, pg. 51
[43] Ibid, pg. 60
[44] Ibid, pg. 63
[45] IDesan, S., & Company, T. (2013). Living the French Revolution and the Age of Napoleon. The Great Courses, pg. 63

of hierarchy and privileges.⁴⁶ Using the social contract theory and the belief in rights, writers like Thomas Pain came about and declared that each generation had the inherent right to make a government for itself, to benefit the generation itself, and that dead men's ideas should not be able to rule a living generation.⁴⁷

When we think about what the French Revolution was really about, we must think of representative government, popular sovereignty, civil rights, and a Catholic religion that is subservient to the secular state; this is the essence of the modern system we are living in today, which came from both the Reformation and French Revolution. Thomas Paine, a leading political philosopher in this new political movement, called the state to support equality, that not the Church but the state should offer poor relief, and that the state should be responsible for public education and offer work for unemployed people, and grant pensions for people who became elderly and those who were veterans.⁴⁸

During pre-revolutionary France, meaning a world that closely resembled the classical world of Christendom, you were not free to do whatever you wanted. A person could not, for example, call others to heresy, do things to destroy morality, etc. With this new view on the Declaration of Rights it allowed people to do whatever they wished, just as long as it did not infringe upon the rights of others. Many revolutionaries believed that a person has absolute sovereignty over their own body and even agreed with suicide because of this belief.⁴⁹

This new emphasis on rights, that government is there to protect people's rights, and that sovereignty belongs to the people, took divinity away from God in a sense and made people quasi-divine.⁵⁰ In classical France, people were not free to commit heresy, corrupt morals, and disturb the social order.

---

⁴⁶Ibid, pg. 112
⁴⁷Ibid
⁴⁸Desan, S., & Company, T. (2013). Living the French Revolution and the Age of Napoleon. The Great Courses, pg. 112
⁴⁹ Kennedy, Emmet. A Cultural History of the French Revolution. New Haven, Yale University Press, 1989, pg. xxv
⁵⁰ Ibid, pg. xxvi

With this new view on rights, they came to the rule and norm that nobody can be disturbed by their opinion and even religious opinions, just as long as their words and opinions did not affect the state nor the rights of others. They believed the state should not get involved in policing people's opinions and religious opinions, and the state should only get involved in what it believes to be abuse.[51]

Because they pushed for universal rights, they believed people are "born free and equal in rights" and that the essence of "liberty consists in the power to do whatever does not harm another" (articles 1 and 4 of the declaration). This included religious liberty. They began to see that Catholicism, being the de facto religion of the state, was a threat to this new liberty. They believed that people could be whatever religion they wanted to be.[52]

Because people started to believe in equal rights for all and religious liberty, they began to question why can't Jews also have equal rights? Some were hesitant to give Jews equal rights because many saw Jews as an issue because they often tended to form "a nation within a nation," they often practiced social and cultural isolation, they often had more children than Gentiles due to being more sexually active than gentiles and married at younger ages.

They also witnessed Jews having a strong apathy, mistrust, and sometimes hatred toward Gentiles, and the fact they often practiced usury against Gentiles sparked mistrust. The Talmud also came up for discussion during this debate about giving rights to Jews and how this book allowed Jews to defraud Christians, who said blasphemous things about Christ. They questioned how they could coexist with the new laws of the country.[53] Eventually, they decided to give equal rights to Jews as well because they stopped putting religion as the sole basis of the

---

[51] Ibid, pg. 147
[52] Ibid, pg. 147-148
[53] Kennedy, Emmet. A Cultural History of the French Revolution. New Haven, Yale University Press, 1989, pg. 74

social order. They created a new social order using rights, popular sovereignty, and liberty.

REVOLUTIONARY CHANGES TO THE FAMILY STRUCTURE

With all these calls for social and political equality along with a strong sense of individualism being discussed and implemented in the new secular society of France, the people started to notice that this equality and individualism did not apply to the way the family was governed in France at this time. The revolutionaries sought to change the family structure. The classical world was built on hierarchy, as we have shown before:

"In the Old Regime—French society before 1789—hierarchy structured every relationship: the king over his subjects, lords over their peasants, men over women, masters over slaves in the colonies, and clergy over laypeople. At the time, even those on the bottom of this structure believed that hierarchy was natural—sanctioned by God."[54]

The Revolution was all about undermining the king and aristocracy and bringing about a sense of egalitarianism. Because family is the microorganism of a state, how it is governed directly reflects how a state is governed. What a child learns during his upbringing in a family directly affects that child's values, beliefs, morals, culture, ideas, practices, etc. For the revolution to take real effect and destroy the classical world, the revolutionaries had to destroy the classical family structure of patriarchy and primogeniture. They reasoned that people were apt to accept a monarchy because they had to obey the patria potestas (male head of household) within the family, who resembled a type of king within the family; for example, they reasoned how an adult son of a family could have the right to vote and be an equal citizen in society, yet had his property managed and his marriage choice controlled by the patria potestas within his family?[55]

---

[54] Desan, S., & Company, T. (2013). Living the French Revolution and the Age of Napoleon. The Great Courses.
[55] Ibid, pg. 154-155

They reasoned that by changing the family structure, undermining the patria potestas, how property was controlled and distributed in the family structure governorship, and how the Catholic religion governed the family, they could undermine and alter the political order by altering the family order. They reasoned that if they could undermine the patria potestas of the family, people would no longer have use for a king. By taking control of the family from the Catholic clergy, they could alter church-state relations, and they were right. Here, they heavily focused on altering the family to mimic revolutionary principles of egalitarianism and purposely undermine the classical social order of Christendom.

Because clergy and the canon law controlled marriage, marriage was looked at as a sacrament and a contract, which, being a sacrament, was controlled by the Catholic Church. Because the patria potestas of the family had to look after the family, meaning he controlled the property, his aim was often to continue the family legacy, ensure the family wealth and name were protected, etc. Here, he would often greatly influence the marriage choices of his children and siblings because marriage was not necessarily based on romantic love as many modern thinkers view it today. It was based on other factors, such as making sure the people under him marry into the same class and social structures to protect wealth, reputation, class, and position in society. Because marriage was a sacrament controlled by canon law, divorce did not exist because canon law saw marriage based on divine revelation to be indissoluble and that no man can rend asunder what God has joined together.

In order to put a knife in the back of the classical family structure, the revolutionaries began to speak against arranged marriages by the patria potestas and condemned the lack of divorce. In order to undermine the patria potestas and the Catholic Church's hold on governing marriage, the revolutionaries called for people's absolute liberty in choosing their spouses, that they should be free to marry who they wish, and they also argued they should be free to marry and divorce at whim.[56]

They sought to undermine the Church fully by redefining marriage only as a civil contract controlled by the new secular state. They no longer viewed it as a sacrament and that every citizen could make or break this contract at whim or will.[57] Instead of looking at marriage as a sacrament, they started to view marriage as being something defined by companionship, love, and affection and that liberty should be linked to free love. They even began to reason that if people could freely love, marry, and divorce whomever they wanted, they would even love each other more.[58] Even though some people argued that divorce was bad for society because it was bad for children and produced social instability and disorder, more people believed in divorce and free love. They simply outnumbered those who believed otherwise.

In September of 1792, the French Revolution assembly passed one of the most liberal divorce laws ever to pass in Western civilization. With these new laws in place, a couple can freely petition the government for divorce if the divorce was based on reasons of insanity, mutual consent, emigration, long-term absence, cruelty, incompatibility, etc.[59] They even made divorce proceedings very cheap and easy by creating new arbitration and family courts. As a blow to the Church and canon law, they even allowed divorced spouses to remarry. They did this all with the intention to mirror the family to the new liberty they sought for society and to undermine the patria potestas (male head of household), the Church controlling marriage, all with the aim for a brand-new secular humanist world order.[60]

---

[56] Desan, S., & Company, T. (2013). Living the French Revolution and the Age of Napoleon. The Great Courses., pg. 155
[57] Ibid
[58] Ibid
[59] Ibid, 156
[60] Ibid

REVOLUTIONARY INHERITANCE LAWS: ENDING PATRIA POTESTAS IN FRANCE

In classical France, more specifically pre-revolution France, property was treated in such a way that empowered the patria potestas. They followed a principle called primogeniture, meaning the property was passed down to the oldest son.[61] This practice ensured that estates remained intact across generations, thereby preserving the wealth and influence of noble families. By consolidating assets under a single heir, primogeniture avoided the fragmentation of property that would have occurred if estates were divided among multiple offspring. This economic stability empowered the patria potestas, the father's absolute authority over the family, by centralizing control and decision-making power within the household.

This centralized family structure mirrored and reinforced the hierarchical nature of the monarchy, where a single ruler held ultimate authority over the state. The stability provided by primogeniture and the patria potestas created a societal framework that aligned people to accept and even support the monarchy, as both systems emphasized continuity, order, and control. Furthermore, primogeniture protected property generationally, ensuring that estates remained significant economic and social units within the noble class, thereby maintaining their status and power over time.

Because the revolutionaries wanted to undermine the monarchy, destroy the nobility, weaken and destroy the traditional system, and seek to promote egalitarianism in society to change the social order, they produced a campaign of books, pamphlets, and any other means to communication to attack the parental authority of the patria potestas. They hit the institution where it hurts the most: the distribution of family property in inheritance. They called to enact laws that would distribute property in inheritance equally. They even sought to give

---

[61]Ibid, pg. 158

illegitimate children a share in inheritance property, wanting to alleviate the stigma associated with bastardy.[62]

The practice of primogeniture contributed to societal stability and family wealth. The practice ensured estates were not broken up, which worked to maintain family wealth across generations. An undivided estate generated more income, raised and kept high family social status, helped raise efficiency and estate management, reinforced hierarchy and stability, reduced disputes, bolstered marital alliances by joining two large undivided estates together, helped protect the family legacy, simplified the legal process for succession, and allowed families to consolidate resources. Family members could rely on large estates, thus lowering the risk of poverty within families because families held on to large estates, allowing the families to maintain their power and influence through the centuries, etc.

Because the revolutionaries wanted to do away with the traditional system entirely and with the monarchy completely, they wanted to do away with the mini-monarch within the family, the patria potestas. In the 1790s, they did just that. They completely abolished primogeniture. Not only that, they took away the power of fathers to imprison disobedient children and wayward wives.[63] They passed laws that forced parents from writing a will favoring one child over the other and that parents had to pass their property and money equally to all children, and even illegitimate children got a share if the father recognized them as his own.[64]

One historian named Lynn Hunt believed that the revolution itself was an attack on fathers in general, meaning that the revolution was a band of brothers who waged a campaign against their father, that once they killed the king, the symbolic and sacred father of the nation, it became possible for take authority away from real fathers themselves.[65] This is because monarchial

---

[62] Desan, S., & Company, T. (2013). Living the French Revolution and the Age of Napoleon. The Great Courses, pg. 158
[63] Ibid
[64] Ibid
[65] Ibid, pg. 159

politics and the classical family mirrored each other; the authority of the father mirrored the authority of the king, and just as the king ruled over the nation, the father ruled over the household, thus reinforcing one another. They saw monarchical society as a type of inequality because it was based on hierarchy; they destroyed this hierarchy in society and saw it as their duty to destroy this hierarchy within the family.

Because they allowed for easy divorce and wanted to destroy the patria potestas completely, they called for free love to make divorce easy. They even argued that this type of free love would make couples happier, and happier couples would produce more children. But the problem was that women initiated "two-thirds to three-quarters of all divorces." The revolutionaries argued that this freedom was important. Still, if their intention was to destroy the patria potestas, there would be no better way than for women to get a divorce easily, thus undermining the power of the patria potestas.

Even putting a further blow on the patriarchy, in 1792, the revolutionary legislature passed a law that allowed for any young man or woman to marry without the consent of their parents; its very intention was to undermine the patriarchal power of the father and to attack the concept of arranged marriages.[66] The revolutionaries had a major problem with parental authority because they wanted to change the social order. They wanted almost absolute unity in society, and they sought to destroy the influence parents had on their children.[67]

---

[66] Desan, S., & Company, T. (2013). Living the French Revolution and the Age of Napoleon. The Great Courses, pg. 156
[67] McManners, John. The French Revolution and the Church. Church Historical Society, 1969, pg. 72

REVOLUTIONARY REFORMS CONCERNING THE PRIVILEGES OF THE ARISTOCRACY

When the revolutionaries started to take over society because they were pushing to destroy feudalism and the Catholic Church's stronghold over the nation, the Revolutionary assembly called on its members to freely give away their privileges. The once-aristocrats were stripped of their privileges.[68] They gave away their privilege of collecting the once seigneurial dues owed to them by the peasants that were paid for centuries, all with the dream of fulfilling this radical concept of egalitarianism. The once aristocratic class, in exchange for their privilege, gave them up for the idea of liberty, peace, equality, and better fraternity to establish a free and popular government and export these ideas outside France.[69] The biggest aspect of aristocratic privilege was freedom from taxation, and they freely gave up these privileges, although based on the pressure the revolutionaries brought upon society, they may have been compelled to give their privileges up. The largest aspect of the revolution was the attack on privilege itself. Most of the common people could not stand the aristocracy being free from taxation; they ended their noble statuses and wanted equality with the nobility, and they sought to end this class in the name of egalitarianism.

In revolutionary France, revolutionaries sought to end aristocratic privileges to promote egalitarianism and dismantle the entrenched social hierarchy that had long oppressed the common people. Key figures like Maximilien Robespierre and other members of the Jacobin Club aimed to abolish feudal rights and noble privileges, seeing them as remnants of an unjust and outdated system. They enacted measures such as the abolition of seigneurial dues and titles of nobility through legislation like the August Decrees of 1789 and the subsequent radical reforms during the Reign of Terror, which aimed to eradicate the influence and economic power of the aristocracy and create a more equitable society. In essence, the revolutionaries hated the nobility and their privileges; they

---

[68] Desan, S., & Company, T. (2013). Living the French Revolution and the Age of Napoleon. The Great Courses, pg. 53
[69] Doyle, W. (2018). The Oxford History of the French Revolution. Oxford University Press, pg. 199

pushed for equality of opportunity and fiscal equality as an alternative to their privilege, ending their statuses completely.[70]

The revolutionaries hated the concept of noble birth, and here, they pushed a merit system opposing the idea of noble birth and status in society. This gave the idea of merit the ability to destroy the concept of nobility and noble status.[71] Through this merit-based push, they got commoners in high-level positions, meaning commoners could now serve as officers in the army, rise to higher positions in the Churches, and hold high government positions.[72]

Classical France was about the separation of classes. Each class had a role to play; the revolutionaries hated the concept of classes because they believed in the radical concept of egalitarianism and social contract. The revolution was based on destroying social classes and bringing people a sense of equality. It meant power sharing amongst all the classes, and in order to achieve this radical vision, they had to destroy the classical system almost in its entirety. Instead of allowing the aristocratic class to decide the fate of the future, they would rather implement the new and radical concept of universal manhood suffrage based on the direct election of the people, no matter what class they belonged to.

---

[70] Kennedy, Emmet. A Cultural History of the French Revolution. New Haven, Yale University Press, 1989, pg. 145
[71] Desan, S., & Company, T. (2013). Living the French Revolution and the Age of Napoleon. The Great Courses, pg. 56
[72] Ibid

THE CATHOLIC CHURCH AND ITS ROLE IN PRE-REVOLUTIONARY FRANCE

In pre-revolutionary France, the Catholic Church and the Pope held significant influence over both the spiritual and temporal affairs of the nation. The Catholic Church was not only a religious institution but also a powerful political and economic entity that shaped the societal structure of the classical regime. In pre-revolutionary society, which the revolutionaries called the "old regime," the maxim when it came to the Church read "Il faut consulter l'église" which translates to "It is necessary to consult the Church," meaning that in matters of doctrine, ethics, and belief, when people and officials sought spiritual and moral counsel, it was necessary to consult the Church.

The Catholic Church wielded considerable power in France, with the Pope at its apex as the supreme spiritual authority. The Church's influence permeated every level of society, from the monarchy to the common people. Although a secular leader, the king of France was deeply intertwined with the Church. The Church often reinforced his legitimacy, which anointed and crowned him in elaborate ceremonies, suggesting divine approval of his rule. This created a symbiotic relationship where the monarchy supported the Church, and in return, the Church endorsed the monarchy.

The Church was one of the largest landowners in France, controlling about 10% of all land. This vast wealth came from tithes, rents from agricultural lands, and donations from the faithful. The revenue generated from these lands and other ecclesiastical activities made the Church an economic powerhouse. This wealth enabled the Church to fund grand cathedrals, maintain a large clerical hierarchy, and wield significant influence over the peasantry, who relied on its charity and spiritual services.

The Church's hierarchical structure, with priests, bishops, and archbishops, ensured its extensive reach and control over French society. Bishops often held significant secular power in addition to their spiritual duties. They could influence local governance, administer justice, and manage educational institutions. Secular leaders, including local lords and officials, frequently found themselves deferring to the Church's authority on various matters, reflecting the Church's pervasive control.

As the spiritual overseer of the nation, the Church regulated moral and ethical standards, shaping public and private life. It controlled key life events such as baptisms, marriages, and funerals, making the Church integral to the social fabric. Additionally, the Church managed education and hospitals, further cementing its role in everyday life. Through sermons, confessions, and other religious practices, priests and bishops could influence the beliefs and behaviors of the populace.

The Catholic Church's roles were multifaceted: it served as a religious authority, a political player, an economic entity, and a provider of social services. The Church promulgated doctrines and provided spiritual guidance, ensuring that Catholicism remained the central tenet of French life. Its clergy were often involved in local administration and governance, blurring the lines between secular and ecclesiastical duties.

The Church's power was not absolute but formidable. Its influence extended through its ability to excommunicate individuals, including kings, which could isolate them politically and socially. The Pope's authority as the ultimate spiritual leader added an international dimension to the Church's influence in France, often complicating the country's internal and external political affairs.

CHAPTER 3:

SUBJUGATING FAITH: THE FRENCH REVOLUTION'S OVERTHROW OF CATHOLIC CHURCH AUTHORITY

Because the revolutionaries wanted to do away with the classical regime to bring about a new society, they saw the pillars of that old regime as monarchy, aristocratic privilege, the Catholic Church, and the Pope. Once they destroyed the monarchy and aristocratic privilege, they focused entirely on subjugating Catholicism to the secular state. The revolutionary assembly sought direct control over the Church; here, the new secular state would pay the salaries of all the clergy in France, and common sense says that the ones who pay you are the ones who have control. Instead of bishops (successors to the Apostles) and the Pope (successor of St. Peter) choosing priests as they had for nearly 1800 years prior to the revolution, the revolutionaries decided that active citizens of the revolution would now elect priests.[73]

They even went further. They compelled priests to take an oath of loyalty to the new regime and revolution. The oath made it clear: either the priest supports the revolution, or they support God and the Pope. The Pope at the time condemned the oath and warned priests against taking it.[74] Not all bishops and priests took the oath; the ones who took the oath were called or known as constitutional clergy, while the clergy who refused to take the oath were called "non-jurors or refractory clergy." The constitutional clergy often saw themselves as a type of citizen-

---

[73] Desan, S., & Company, T. (2013). Living the French Revolution and the Age of Napoleon. The Great Courses, pg. 85
[74] Ibid

priest, and the non-jurors saw themselves as uncorrupted servants of God.[75]

When bishops denounced the new Constitution, they were almost always dismissed. When they could not dismiss all the priests who refused to take the oath, they stopped their salaries, and the oath was the test to get their salaries continued in some cases.[76] When a clergy member sought to be elected to a benefice, one of the requirements was to take the oath.[77] Bishops in pre-revolutionary France were nominated by the head of state upon the approval of the Pope, and the tithe and other forms of support usually paid them. They had the spiritual authority given directly to them by the Pope. During and after the Revolution, they were paid by the state, meaning the new secular state took control of them.[78]

Many people were suspicious of both the constitutional clergy and the non-juror clergy, depending on whether they supported the revolution or were sympathetic to the pre-revolutionary regime. In areas where non-juror priests dominated, the people often saw the constitutional clergy as a type of usurper, and non-juror clergy, in the beginning, were often seen as a type of hero. Many constitutional clergymen saw the revolution as a type of God's work because they believed egalitarianism was closer to the spirit of Christianity than the old social order of society.[79]

The non-juror priests were, by the revolutionaries, often seen as traitors to the Revolution, and many revolutionaries were ready to lead riots to disperse their congregations. They used the oath as a test of loyalty to the nation and patriotism itself.[80] Many non-juror priests were under heavy surveillance, and some were being imprisoned. They even whipped women who mocked constitutional priests[81]. The revolutionaries proposed ending the

---

[75] Ibid
[76] Doyle, W. (2018). The Oxford History of the French Revolution. Oxford University Press, pg. 144
[77] Ibid, pg. 145
[78] Ibid, pg. 390
[79] Desan, S., & Company, T. (2013). Living the French Revolution and the Age of Napoleon. The Great Courses, pg. 86
[80] McManners, John. The French Revolution and the Church. Church Historical Society, 1969, pg. 61
[81] Ibid, pg. 62

salary of non-juror priests, reasoning that we should not pay our enemies to wage war upon us.[82] Before the revolutionaries began to take over the Church, the Church, through the tithe, freedom from taxation, donations, and other dues, was rather rich. With this wealth, they were able to operate in the ways explained before. Now, they were being salaried by the secular state, and the revolutionaries declared that the clerics should be happy with the salary the new secular state offered them.[83]

Even before the Revolution, there was some backlash against the power of the Church. There were certain protocols that excluded the Pope from intervening between the king and the clergy, that canons of councils could not be published without royal approval, and that churchmen could not be judged outside the jurisdiction of the kingdom.[84] Yet despite these setbacks, the Church gained significant footing in being of the moral leadership of the kingdom.[85]

The revolutionaries were setting up a separate secular culture. For example, in July 1791, they made a procession to honor the once Voltaire (one of the revolutionary founders of the ideology of the revolution), as they brought his remains to the Patheon to bury him in a public place as a type of secular honoring, there was no priest, no blessing, and no religious element, and no references to a Catholic God, this was all done purposely as a symbolic act to show the world that they are creating a secular culture free of Catholicism.[86] They even created festivals of reason to replace religious festivals.

They created the Festival of Reason and held the festival inside the Cathedral of Notre Dame, which is dedicated to philosophy; they adorned it with sculptures of philosophers and created an image of a lady in place of Mother Mary as the goddess of reason. During this time, there was a national push to close churches, compel priests to resign, and openly use

---

[82] McManners, John. The French Revolution and the Church. Church Historical Society, 1969, pg. 63
[83] Doyle, W. (2018). The Oxford History of the French Revolution. Oxford University Press, pg. 136
[84] McManners, John. The French Revolution and the Church. Church Historical Society, 1969, pg. 5
[85] Ibid
[86] Desan, S., & Company, T. (2013). Living the French Revolution and the Age of Napoleon. The Great Courses, pg. 86

blasphemy to chase religion away, as in doing acts of sacrilege; they destroyed images and statues of saints, melted down sacred objects, guzzled communion wine, dressed up a donkey as bishops to humiliate them, etc.[87]

They began to turn down closed churches as storehouses for weapons, even places to store grain, and even turned them into stables for horses.[88] As a further attack on the Church and the growing suspicion of non-juror priests, by the belief that they were forming a counterrevolution, the revolutionary assembly passed a law that if 20 citizens denounced any non-juror priest, that non-juror priest would face deportation.[89] They began to complain that priests were like parasites and that they should make them useful to the nation. Here, they pushed many to resign and disavow their vow of celibacy and get married. They further pressured priests to take the oath of allegiance, and if they did not, they would be threatened with deportation and/or imprisonment.

Because they viewed non-juror priests with suspicion for not taking the oath, they began to arrest them; they often deported them or restricted their place of domicile.[90] Many priests had to go underground to continue their work free from the tyranny of the new secular regime. The revolutionaries then devised a new oath, and if the priests refused to take it, they lost their place and pension. As an act of further subjugation, if six citizens now denounced any priest, this made their deportation automatic.[91] The oath read, "I swear to be faithful to the Nation, to maintain with all my power, Liberty, Equality, the security of persons and property, and to die, if need be, for the execution of the law."[92] The problem was that the clergy depended upon their pensions, and if they refused the oath, their pensions would stop and starve. However, taking the oath meant the end of the classical

---

[87] Ibid, pg. 150-151
[88] Ibid, pg. 151
[89] Desan, S., & Company, T. (2013). Living the French Revolution and the Age of Napoleon. The Great Courses, pg. 125
[90] McManners, John. The French Revolution and the Church. Church Historical Society, 1969, pg. 65
[91] Ibid
[92] McManners, John. The French Revolution and the Church. Church Historical Society, 1969, pg. 65

church in France, and a newly subjugated church came as a result.

When the revolutionaries drafted the Declaration of the Rights of Man and Citizen, they obviously refused to declare Catholicism the official state religion. They refused to restrict freedom of expression. In other words, they refused to stop heresy and that civil rights were open to all; this meant the Protestants, even Jews, enjoyed the same rights. When clerical speakers came to speak to the assembly, they were heckled away, and this is when they started to conspire to take the lands away from the Catholic Church entirely.[93] On February 13, 1790, they shut down all Catholic monasteries and convents, except the ones that were dedicated to education and work involving some charitable interest.

They forbade religious vows and took their property away along with their income.[94] The revolutionaries often believed that closing down the convents was doing the nuns a favor, yet France's 45,000 nuns were almost unanimously against the closure of the convents.[95] Because the revolutionaries did not believe in the sacraments and the sanctification of the soul, they viewed monasteries and convents as useless to the nation and revolution, and because they lived on donations, they saw them as parasites. They started to question what a monk does for a living. They would often say he is a fool who binds himself to an oath and lives off the fruits of others.[96] They believed monks were unsuited to educate the citizens because they viewed monks as fools and parasites.[97]

In order to destroy the relationship between the state and the Pope, instead of the Pope and bishops appointing priests, they had the laity choose the new constitutional priests. When it came to the bishops, who were supposed to be successors of the Apostles appointed by the Pope, the successor of St. Peter,

---

[93] Desan, S., & Company, T. (2013). Living the French Revolution and the Age of Napoleon. The Great Courses, pg. 137
[94] Doyle, W. (2018). The Oxford History of the French Revolution. Oxford University Press, pg. 137
[95] Doyle, W. (2018). The Oxford History of the French Revolution. Oxford University Press, pg. 398
[96] McManners, John. The French Revolution and the Church. Church Historical Society, 1969, pg. 9
[97] McManners, John. The French Revolution and the Church. Church Historical Society, 1969, pg. 10

bishops were now chosen by departmental assemblies.[98] In order to cut off the nation from the Pope and Vatican, all French citizens were forbidden to have any contact with any foreign bishop or anyone associated with a foreign bishop. The Pope was the one who was supposed to at least confirm episcopal appointments, and now he was simply notified that someone was appointed.[99]

BREAKING ECCLESIASTICAL POWER: SECULAR EDUCATION, HOSPITALS AND POOR RELIEF

Before the French Revolution, the Catholic Church wielded significant influence over many aspects of daily life in France, notably in the realms of education, poor relief, and healthcare. The Church's control over these sectors stemmed from both historical precedent and its deeply entrenched position within society. The Church had been a cornerstone of European civilization for centuries, and its role in education and social welfare was a natural extension of its religious mission to provide for the spiritual and physical needs of the populace.

The Church's involvement in education was profound. Monasteries, convents, and cathedral schools were among the primary institutions where children and young adults received their education. The clergy and religious orders were responsible for the curriculum, which often centered around religious instruction but included reading, writing, and basic arithmetic. These institutions were pivotal in a society where formal education was not widespread, offering few opportunities for literacy and learning. The Church's educational role was supported by tithes, donations, and endowments from the faithful, ensuring that it had the resources to maintain its schools and employ teachers.

Similarly, the Catholic Church played a crucial role in providing poor relief and healthcare. Many hospitals and hospices were founded and run by religious orders, offering care

---
[98] Doyle, W. (2018). The Oxford History of the French Revolution. Oxford University Press, pg. 137
[99] Doyle, W. (2018). The Oxford History of the French Revolution. Oxford University Press, pg. 141

to the sick, the poor, and the elderly. The Church saw this as part of its mission to practice charity and to serve those in need, aligning with its teachings on compassion and service. This role was supported by the same financial means that sustained its educational endeavors, including alms, bequests, and the voluntary contributions of the laity. The Church's infrastructure for poor relief included distributing food and clothing, sheltering the homeless, and providing basic medical care, which was especially vital in a period when the state lacked such organized systems.

The Catholic Church's control over education, poor relief, and healthcare greatly elevated its importance within French society. It was not just a spiritual leader but also a crucial provider of essential social services. This multifaceted role reinforced the Church's authority and influence, as the clergy were seen as both moral and practical leaders. The benefits of this arrangement were significant for many individuals who relied on the Church's services for survival and education. It fostered a sense of community and provided a social safety net in an era when such support was otherwise scarce.

The revolutionaries began to focus on education and believed it needed to be regenerated to fit the ideals of the revolution. The problem was that because the revolutionaries stopped the tithe from being collected and donations to monasteries were no longer being collected, the money the Church once received was drying up. The Catholic teachers who refused to take the oath were being dismissed, and Catholic education itself became in the crosshairs of the revolution.[100] In the old regime, certain groups, such as aristocrats, had more access to higher forms of education than others. Despite this, the revolutionaries used education to destroy even the idea of the old regime. They used education as a means to create people who appeal to reason and who would be patriotic and ready to partake in the nation's politics. Here, the new secular state hired teachers to teach basic reading, math, and writing, along with the political principles of

---

[100] Ibid, pg. 400-401

the new secular state, the new republic's morals, and a sense of purging nearly everything from the old regime.[101]

Because the revolutionaries hated the Catholic Church and desired to destroy the old regime by whatever means necessary, they focused on education to do just that. They knew that education was under the control of the Catholic Church for centuries, and it reinforced Catholic hegemony over society and taught the feudal system. They used education to remake a new type of citizen freed from all the traditional ways pre-revolutionary France operated. This is where they came up with a new educational institution that was secular, free, and open to both males and females.[102]

As a blow to the power of the Church, which once oversaw hospitals, in 1794, all hospital property was nationalized, a nice term for saying the property was stolen by the state and taken over by the state.[103] The hospitals, once under the control of the Catholic Church, were able to fund the hospitals through tithe, donations, and other endowments. Once the new secular state took over the hospitals and stopped the tithe, they supported the secular hospitals through local taxes and surcharges on luxuries, like theater tickets.[104]

---

[101] Doyle, W. (2018). The Oxford History of the French Revolution. Oxford University Press, pg. 224
[102] Ibid, pg. 198
[103] Ibid, pg. 402
[104] Ibid

SECULAR REBELLION: HOW FREEDOM OF CONSCIENCE CONFRONTED CATHOLIC HEGEMONY

Since classical church doctrine is upon the Petrine Doctrine, that the apostolic church is the Church that Jesus started upon the rock of St. Peter, that church is most definitely the Catholic Church, which to this day has an unbroken succession of Popes and bishops since St. Peter and the Apostles. Classical society was built upon this religion, being the only religion of the state, and the heresies and sects had no legal right to exist. Classical society could not give equal rights to Jews and Protestants because Jews were often seen as rejectors of Christ and were known to make a nation within a nation, separating themselves from the common laity. Protestantism is a heresy that rejected the Pope and the priesthood, rejected the Catholic Church as the sole interpreter of scripture, and spread the heretical doctrines of sola scriptura, sola fide, sola gratia, etc. (refer to the upcoming book on Protestantism for a full explanation).

Here, the revolutionaries, as a blow to the Catholic Church, gave citizenship to Jews and opened all offices to Protestants. They even lifted the press censorship in matters of religion and morals, which worked to guard the morality and spirituality of society for many years before that.[105] The idea of freedom of conscience came to light during this time, and the concept of toleration came about, and the notion that differences in religion and opinions are not crimes took root.[106] Before the assembly passed this decree, one patriotic priest got up. He said, "Son culte sera seul autorisé," meaning his religion was to be the only one authorized, meaning that Catholicism was the state religion with the exclusive right in public worship. Yet, the assembly refused to consent and reasoned that they had no right over the consciences of men, and the assembly committed apostasy against Catholicism.[107] They ended up using freedom of conscience as a weapon against the power of the Church, which worked to flood

---

[105] McManners, John. The French Revolution and the Church. Church Historical Society, 1969, pg. 25-26
[106] Ibid, pg. 10
[107] McManners, John. The French Revolution and the Church. Church Historical Society, 1969, pg. 26

society with heresy to the point where people could no longer, for the most part, recognize truth from untruth.

DESECRATED DOMAINS: THE NATIONALIZATION OF CHURCH PROPERTY& AND THE ABOLITION OF THE TITHE

In prerevolutionary France, the Catholic Church was one of the largest landowners in the country, controlling approximately 10% of all land. This vast wealth in land holdings bolstered the Church's power significantly, enabling it to wield immense influence over French society and politics. The Church's estates generated substantial income through rents and agricultural produce, which funded its religious, educational, and charitable activities, further entrenching its authority and presence in everyday life. The extensive land ownership by the Church also provided it with a network of power and loyalty among the populace, as many peasants and tenants depended on the Church for their livelihoods.

As the French Revolution unfolded, the revolutionary government viewed the Church's vast land holdings as both a symbol of the "old regime" and a practical resource to address the nation's financial crisis. In a radical move, the National Assembly decreed the nationalization of Church lands in 1789, effectively seizing these properties and bringing them under state control. This expropriation was justified on the grounds that the land belonged to the nation and could be better utilized for the public good. The confiscated Church lands were auctioned off, often to the bourgeoisie and peasants, thereby redistributing wealth and land ownership in a manner that aimed to undermine the old feudal structures.

The nationalization of Church lands also facilitated the introduction of France's first paper currency, known as assignats. The revolutionary government issued these assignments and was backed by the value of the expropriated Church properties. Initially conceived as a solution to the country's dire financial straits, the assignats helped finance the revolutionary activities and provide liquidity in a period of economic turmoil. However, their over-issuance eventually led to inflation and depreciation, contributing to economic instability.

The expropriation of Church lands and the issuance of assignats had profound effects on the power of the Catholic Church in France. The Church's loss of land deprived it of its economic base, significantly reducing its financial independence and societal influence. This weakening of the Church's material power was accompanied by broader anti-clerical measures, including the Civil Constitution of the Clergy, which sought to bring the Church under state control. During and after the revolution, the Church's role in French society was irrevocably altered, as its former dominance gave way to a new secular order that prioritized state sovereignty and egalitarian principles. This shift marked the beginning of a prolonged struggle between the Church and the state, a legacy of the revolutionary upheavals that reshaped the contours of French society.

Since the revolutionaries wanted to put the Church under state control, what better way than to take its vast amount of land? Here, during a vote in the Assembly, the majority voted to seize church lands and made a declaration that those lands belonged to the nation. As a further blow to the Catholic Church, as written before, the secular state was now in charge of paying the clergy, and the new secular state took over the care for the poor and needy.[108] In order to fully conquer and subjugate the Church to the new secular state, by making the clergy dependent on the regime for its salary and taking church lands, they ensured that the clergy was separated from their "old way of life," and this made sure they had an interest in the revolution.[109]

In prerevolutionary France, the tithe was a compulsory levy imposed on agricultural produce, typically amounting to one-tenth of a farmer's harvest. Instituted by the Catholic Church, the tithe was designed to fund the Church's extensive religious, charitable, and social activities. These funds were crucial for maintaining churches, supporting the clergy, and providing for the poor and sick. The tithe represented a significant source of income for the Church, underpinning its economic power and

---

[108] McManners, John. The French Revolution and the Church. Church Historical Society, 1969, pg. 25-27
[109] Ibid, pg. 29

enabling it to play a central role in the daily lives of the French populace.

The tithe was rooted in biblical tradition and had been an established practice for centuries. Its collection and utilization were structured to ensure that religious services could be sustained, church buildings maintained, and various charitable functions carried out. The revenues from the tithe were also used to support parish priests and other clergy, who in turn provided spiritual guidance, education, and other services to their communities. While essential for the Church's operations, the tithe system was often resented by the rural population, who saw it as an additional burden on top of other feudal dues and taxes.

The French Revolution brought about a dramatic shift in attitudes toward traditional institutions, including the Church. Revolutionary leaders viewed the tithe as an emblem of the Church's feudal privileges and an unjust burden on the peasantry. In 1789, the National Assembly decided to abolish the tithe as part of a broader effort to dismantle feudal structures and redistribute power and resources more equitably. This decision was motivated by a desire to relieve the rural population of oppressive levies and to weaken the financial and social influence of the Church, which was seen as a pillar of the classical regime.

The abolition of the tithe had profound implications for the Church in France. Deprived of a major source of income, the Church struggled to maintain its operations and fulfill its traditional roles. The loss of tithe revenues, combined with the nationalization of Church lands, significantly reduced the Church's economic base and independence. This financial weakening was accompanied by a broader secularization campaign, which sought to reduce the Church's influence in public life and promote state control over religious affairs.

The end of the tithe system marked a turning point in the relationship between the Church and the state in France. It not only alleviated the financial burdens on the rural populace but also symbolized the revolutionary commitment to equality and the dismantling of the old feudal order. The Church's diminished financial power and the state's increasing intervention in religious matters reshaped the religious landscape of France, leading to a more secular society and setting the stage for ongoing conflicts over the role of religion in public life.

The tithe was the lifeblood of the Church; it is what sustained their operations. With the tithe being ended and church lands taken, the Church could no longer remain the once powerful institution it was. The truth is the revolutionaries hated Christianity and did nearly everything they could do to take it out of society, or at best, to weaken it as much as they could. It got so bad for the Church during the revolution that priests were compelled to completely abandon the priesthood. There was rampant destruction of churches during this time. The revolutionaries even made up a new calendar that was not based on religion but on secular principles and even got rid of Sundays and Saints' days.[110]

REVOLUTIONARY ATTACKS ON MONASTICISM AND THE TAKING OF VOWS

Monasticism was a cornerstone of the Catholic Church's spiritual and social fabric in pre-revolutionary France. Monasteries and convents dotted the landscape, serving as centers of prayer, education, and charity. Monks and nuns took vows of poverty, chastity, and obedience, dedicating their lives to religious service and communal living. These vows symbolized a profound commitment to spiritual ideals, often involving a renunciation of worldly possessions and personal ambitions. Monastic communities were influential in preserving religious traditions, promoting learning, and providing social services such as caring for the sick and poor.

The nature of monasticism in France was deeply intertwined with the Church's broader role in society. Monasteries owned vast tracts of land, contributing to the Church's economic power and ability to sustain its religious missions. Monastic lands were typically well-managed and productive, further enhancing the economic stability and influence of these religious institutions.

---

[110] McManners, John. The French Revolution and the Church. Church Historical Society, 1969, pg. 85

The daily life of monks and nuns was governed by strict rules and routines centered around prayer, work, and study, reflecting a disciplined and ascetic lifestyle aimed at spiritual enlightenment and service to God.

During the French Revolution, the revolutionary government viewed monasticism with increasing suspicion and hostility. The decision to wipe out monasticism and outlaw the taking of vows stemmed from several key motivations. Revolutionary leaders perceived monastic communities as bastions of feudal privilege and reactionary forces, inherently opposed to the revolutionary ideals of liberty, equality, and fraternity. The Church's substantial landholdings, much of which were monastic properties, were seen as resources that could be better utilized for the public good. Additionally, the celibacy and communal living of monks and nuns were at odds with the revolutionary emphasis on individual freedom and the family as the cornerstone of the new social order.

In 1790, the National Assembly passed the Civil Constitution of the Clergy to bring the Church under state control and diminish its traditional privileges. This was followed by a series of decrees that dissolved monastic orders, confiscated their properties, and prohibited the taking of religious vows. Monastic buildings were repurposed for various secular uses, including schools, hospitals, and military barracks. Many monks and nuns were forced to return to secular life, while others faced persecution or fled abroad.

The abolition of monasticism during the revolution marked a significant transformation in French religious and social life. The eradication of these religious communities was not merely an economic measure but also a symbolic act aimed at dismantling the old order and establishing a secular, rational society. The legacy of this revolutionary policy had enduring effects on the relationship between the Church and the state in France, setting the stage for a secularization process that would continue to evolve in the centuries that followed. Understanding monasticism and its suppression during this period provides critical insight into the profound societal changes unleashed by the French Revolution.

Even though the revolutionaries reasoned that taking church lands and monasteries was economical, reasoning that these lands could be better used to wipe out the national deficit, they sought to subjugate the Catholic Church to the state. Even though this attack appeared to be financial, it was mostly ideological. They wanted the ideals of the revolution to win out throughout the land and wanted no opposition, and the Church stood in the way. Here, they simply gutted the power of the Church in almost every way they could think of.[111]

The issue here was that the revolutionaries were inspired by Voltaire's utilitarianism. Since they did not believe in the sanctification of the soul and the sacraments, they did not like the wealth the monastic order had and viewed the monks' and nuns' spiritual lives based on vows as a type of idleness that did not serve the nation, they believed the monks and nuns would be better of repudiating their vows, marrying, having children, and working for the nation.[112] On February 13, 1790, a law was passed to abolish all religious vows, and every religious order they found that the secular state did not find useful to the nation was dissolved.[113] Instead of worshipping God and God's sovereignty, they called the nation to worship three goddesses: the goddesses of equality, reason, and liberty.[114]

---

[111] McManners, John. The French Revolution and the Church. Church Historical Society, 1969, pg. 31
[112] Ibid
[113] Kennedy, Emmet. A Cultural History of the French Revolution. New Haven, Yale University Press, 1989, pg. 148
[114] McManners, John. The French Revolution and the Church. Church Historical Society, 1969, pg. 101

BEFORE AND AFTER: FRANCE'S RELATIONSHIP WITH THE PAPACY THROUGH THE REVOLUTION

The French Revolution, a period of radical social and political upheaval, marked a decisive break with the traditional structures of power and authority in France. Among the most profound changes was the revolution's rebellion against the classical Catholic society, particularly in its dealings with the Pope. Before the revolution, the Pope held a revered and influential position in France. As the spiritual overseer of the nation, the Pope's authority was intertwined with the monarchy and the societal hierarchy, providing moral guidance and legitimizing the divine right of kings. French society benefited immensely from this relationship, enjoying a cohesive and unified religious identity that permeated every aspect of life, from education to charity, and provided a sense of stability and continuity.

The Pope's influence extended beyond spiritual matters, often playing a crucial role in political decisions and maintaining the social order. The Catholic Church, under the Pope's guidance, operated numerous institutions that offered social services, education, and care for the poor, creating a network of support that reinforced the Church's centrality in daily life. This symbiotic relationship between the French state and the papacy exemplified the classical Catholic society's ethos, where spiritual and temporal powers were closely linked, each reinforcing the other's authority.

However, the revolutionaries saw the papal influence as a cornerstone of the classical regime that needed to be dismantled. The revolutionary government systematically weakened the Pope's influence, beginning with the Civil Constitution of the Clergy in 1790, which sought to bring the Church under state control. Clergy were required to swear allegiance to the new regime, effectively severing their ties with the Pope. The revolutionaries confiscated church lands, disrupted traditional religious practices, and propagated secular ideologies to undermine the Church's power.

As the revolution intensified, the Pope himself became a target. Pope Pius VI was arrested and taken into French custody, a dramatic move that symbolized the revolution's break with the old order. The Pope's arrest and subsequent death in captivity highlighted the revolution's determination to dismantle the traditional Catholic power structures. The loss of the papal states further diminished the Pope's temporal power and paved the way for a new, secular society. The Pope suffered immensely because he refused to give up his temporal authority and refused French demands from the revolutionaries. Because of this, he was arrested and imprisoned by French forces under Napoleon. He eventually died in exile in Valence, France, on August 29, 1799.

The revolutionaries hated the idea of spiritual oversight of the nation; they wanted complete liberty to do whatever they pleased and did not want anything to stand in their way of making a society of secular supremacy. One of the ways they started to diminish the power of the Pope before French society invaded Italy and arrested the Pope was by forbidding bishops from communicating with Rome in their confirmation of their appointments.[115] This was a major blow to the hierarchical and unified structure of the Church because a bishop being confirmed by the Pope meant they were aligned with the doctrinal and spiritual authority of the papacy. Bishops being in union with the papacy was a sure way to maintain the integrity of church doctrine. It prevented heresy and schisms, and papal approval helped bring legitimacy to their office of bishop.

Often, bishops acted as intermediaries between church and state relations. When bishops were confirmed by the Pope and had close relations with the Pope, this ensured expedient church and state relations and entirely reinforced a Catholic global identity in Christendom. The state cutting bishops off from the Pope, made bishops lose legitimacy, allowed the revolutionaries to choose bishops who supported their ideas, and destroyed the Church's autonomy, which enabled it to be a spiritual oversight; it eroded people's allegiance to the Pope and forced people to align with the state and their new ideas. Overall, this revolution

---

[115] Kennedy, Emmet. A Cultural History of the French Revolution. New Haven, Yale University Press, 1989, pg. 150

was about a shift in power and power that was taken from the Pope in order to start a new secular society.

The erosion of the Pope's influence in France had profound implications. It marked the end of the Church's dominance over French political and social life and heralded the rise of secularism. The revolution's actions set a precedent for the separation of church and state, fundamentally altering the relationship between religion and government in France and inspiring similar movements across Europe. The French Revolution's rebellion against the classical Catholic society not only reshaped France but also reverberated throughout the continent, forever changing the landscape of European governance and religious influence.

THE IMPACT OF DE-CHRISTIANIZATION ON REVOLUTIONARY FRANCE'S RELIGIOUS LANDSCAPE

Not only did the revolutionaries completely subjugate the Church to the new secular state, but they also did not stop there on the de-Christianization campaign. They did numerous things. With a burning hatred against Catholicism, they pulled down statutes and columns in churches and destroyed them, and even executed laws that called for the destruction of monuments in churches.[116] Instead of the worship of God prevailing in the land, the revolutionaries worshiped the ideas of liberty. They "desacralized" the Catholic Church and "rebaptized" it as a republican temple, and instead of God being the true sovereign represented by the Pope and his bishops and the king sworn to uphold the interests of the Church, the people themselves were the new sovereigns, the people themselves became sacred characters, and the people must now bow down to man in this new quasi-divine status, instead of worshiping God, man now worships himself.[117] This massive de-Christianization campaign the revolutionaries implemented basically suspended religious practices in France. For nearly ten years, nobody was baptized,

---

[116] Kennedy, Emmet. A Cultural History of the French Revolution. New Haven, Yale University Press, 1989, pg. 204
[117] Ibid, pg. 281

feast days and religious holidays were banned, they even abolished Sunday and the normal Sunday leisure, and there was a cease and desist initiative in the ordination of the priesthood.[118] This was one of the worst attacks on the Church in human history that altered the entire political landscape of the world.

REVOLUTIONARY SECULARIZATION: THE TAKEOVER OF PARISH REGISTERS AND ITS IMPACT

For centuries, the Church held a pivotal role in the documentation of marriages, births, and deaths through the parish register. This practice was not merely an administrative duty but a reflection of the Church's influence over societal structures and personal milestones. Recording these vital events allowed the Church to maintain its central position in community life, ensuring that religious rites and moral oversight were integrated into the most significant moments of an individual's life. This control was crucial for the Church's spiritual and social authority, as it reinforced the interdependence between the Church and the populace, guiding moral conduct and community norms.

The advent of the French Revolution brought about radical changes, including the secularization of the parish registers. The revolutionary state, driven by Enlightenment ideals and a desire to diminish the Church's power, took control of these records. This shift was emblematic of the broader push to reduce the Church's influence and promote a secular society. The revolutionaries effectively removed a key aspect of the Church's authority by transferring the responsibility of recording marriages, births, and deaths to the state. This transition was not only a symbolic act but also a practical reformation, as it centralized vital records under state jurisdiction, reinforcing the separation of church and state.

Control over these records allowed the revolutionary state to redefine marriage as a civil institution rather than a sacramental one, thereby diminishing ecclesiastical control over personal and

---

[118] Ibid, pg. 387

familial matters. This redefinition enabled the state to extend marriage rights and legal recognition to Protestants, Jews, and other religious minorities who had previously been marginalized under the Church's dominion. By secularizing the recording of life events, the revolutionary government facilitated freedom of religion, promoting equality and inclusivity within society. This move was instrumental in ushering in a new era of civil rights, where religious affiliation no longer dictated one's legal standing or social legitimacy. Through these measures, the revolutionary state not only curtailed the Church's dominance but also laid the groundwork for a more pluralistic and secular society.

When parish priests were responsible for recording the crucial points in life in the Parish Register, such as birth, marriage, and death, they were responsible for recording these things, showing that the Church represented both church and state.[119] When the secular state took over the parish register, they took control of civil recordkeeping from the Church and gave it to elected secular government officials. This means that secular elected government officials, not the Church, were responsible for recording life's most important events. At first, a person may think this is a trivial matter. Still, it marked one of the most important shifts in church-state relations in history and transferred authority on life's most important events to a secular authority. This gave the new secular state immense powers and immensely took power away from the Catholic Church. This enabled the new secular government the validity and authority they needed to alter marriage and family, which now gave them the power to recognize Protestant and Jewish marriages.

This gave the new secular government the power to legitimize marriage. Before then, you needed the Church to legitimize your marriage. Now, after the takeover, people needed the secular state to legitimize marriage, and the secular state had the power over marriage and not the Church.[120] When the secular state took over the register, it was not the sacraments that defined citizens;

---

[119] Desan, S., & Company, T. (2013). Living the French Revolution and the Age of Napoleon. The Great Courses, pg. 182
[120] Ibid, pg. 157

it became a choice of who wanted the sacraments to define them. With this new power, the secular state could then control marriage. Instead of marriage being a sacrament and indissoluble, they then allowed for divorce by mutual consent and all other kinds of reforms that the secularists wanted.[121]

THE CHURCH BESIEGED: CATHOLIC CLERGY AND THE FRENCH REVOLUTION'S TERROR

The French Revolution's Reign of Terror marked a period of intense persecution for the Catholic clergy. As revolutionary fervor gripped France, the clergy found themselves targeted by radical elements within the new regime. The revolutionaries, driven by a desire to dismantle the old order and eliminate perceived threats to their nascent secular state, viewed the Catholic Church as a symbol of feudalism and royalist sympathies. As a result, priests, bishops, and other religious figures became victims of systematic violence and oppression. These men and women of the cloth, who had once enjoyed positions of respect and authority, were now vilified, imprisoned, and executed in large numbers.

The suffering of the Catholic clergy was widespread across revolutionary France. From the bustling streets of Paris to the remote countryside, no region was spared from the anti-clerical zeal that swept the nation. Clergy members were often arrested, subjected to mock trials, and sentenced to death by guillotine or other brutal methods. Many were forced into hiding, abandoning their parishes and flocks to escape the relentless persecution. Churches and monasteries were looted, desecrated, and repurposed for secular uses, symbolizing the profound shift in societal values and the diminishing power of the Church.

This wave of anti-clericalism was inspired by Enlightenment ideals and a fierce commitment to the revolutionary principles of liberty, equality, and fraternity. The revolutionaries aimed to eradicate the influence of the Church, which they believed perpetuated ignorance, inequality, and allegiance to the old

---

[121] Kennedy, Emmet. A Cultural History of the French Revolution. New Haven, Yale University Press, 1989, pg. 155

regime. By targeting the clergy, they sought to weaken the Church's hold on French society and pave the way for a new secular state. This persecution of the clergy not only aimed to sever the ties between church and state but also to instill a new civic religion centered around the nation and its revolutionary ideals.

"The worst savageries were in zones of the civil war; 135 priests and monks were massacred in Lyon in November 1793; eighty-three were shot in one day at the Champ des Martyrs near Angers. The bitter details of Carrier's mass drownings at Nantes are well-known...both Carrier and the Revolutionary Tribunal – of the 850 priests (from the North and East and Belgium) imprisoned in the three old slaving ships, only 274 survived...the thirty-two nuns executed by the Commission d'Orange...of the seven Parisian nuns guillotined from May to Joly 1794, three had refused to reveal their the identity of the refractory priest who had been saying their masses, one had been concealing the papers of a refractory, one had corresponded with her émigré brother, another had been found in possession of royalist tracts..."[122]

Nothing pleased the revolutionaries more during the Terror than a priest abjuring his vocation, a priest marrying because of fear. These acts were seen as symbolic victories over the old order, representing the capitulation of religious authority to the revolutionary cause. When priests renounced their clerical duties or entered into marriages, it was a public declaration of the erosion of ecclesiastical power and the triumph of revolutionary ideals. Such capitulations were celebrated as evidence that the grip of the Church on French society was weakening, paving the way for the establishment of a secular state.

These forced conversions and coerced marriages were not only personal humiliations for the clergy involved but also served as powerful propaganda tools for the revolutionaries, reinforcing their narrative of liberation from the oppressive structures of the past. As more priests succumbed to these pressures, the

---

[122] McManners, John. The French Revolution and the Church. Church Historical Society, 1969, pg. 107

authority of the Catholic Church was further eroded, contributing to a broader societal shift toward secularism and rationalism. This shift was integral to the revolutionaries' vision of a new France, where religious dogma was supplanted by Enlightenment principles and the power of the state reigned supreme.

The impact of this persecution on both the Church and French society was profound. The Church's authority and influence were severely undermined, leading to a significant decline in religious practice and the disruption of traditional community structures. This vacuum allowed the revolutionary government to assert greater control over societal norms and institutions, further entrenching the secular state. The repression of the Catholic clergy, therefore, was not merely an act of violence but a strategic effort to reshape French society, diminish the role of religion, and reinforce the revolutionary ethos of the new republic.

REDEFINING TIME: HOW THE FRENCH REVOLUTION CREATED A NEW CALENDAR

As the French Revolution sought to dismantle the old societal structures and establish a new secular state, one of its boldest and most symbolic moves was the creation of a new calendar. In an audacious effort to reinvent French culture from its very foundations, the revolutionaries decided to replace the Gregorian calendar, which had been inextricably linked with the Catholic Church and its religious observances. The Gregorian calendar marked time from the birth of Christ and was deeply intertwined with the liturgical rhythm of Christian holidays. By contrast, the revolutionaries envisioned a calendar structured around the principles of science and republican politics, free from religious connotations.

The new calendar, known as the Republican Calendar, began with Year I on September 22, 1792, the date of the proclamation of the French Republic. This change was not merely a chronological adjustment but a declaration of the new era of rationalism and secular governance. To further distance the populace from the Church, the revolutionaries introduced a ten-day week called a "decade," eliminating the traditional seven-day week that culminated on Sunday, a day of religious observance. This new structure disrupted not only religious practices but also secular routines, such as market days and work schedules.

In addition to removing Sundays, Christmas, Lent, Easter, and saints' days from the calendar, the revolutionaries instituted new festivals designed to commemorate revolutionary events and inculcate patriotic virtues. These festivals were intended to foster a sense of civic pride and loyalty to the Republic, replacing the religious fervor that had once unified the nation. However, this radical reorganization of time proved instantly controversial. It alienated many who were accustomed to the traditional rhythms of life, thereby challenging both secular and religious habits.

Despite its controversy, the Republican Calendar was a powerful tool for the revolutionaries. By redefining time itself, they sought to sever the cultural and temporal ties that bound the people to the Church, thereby weakening the Church's influence and reinforcing the authority of the secular state.

Through this dramatic reimagining of the calendar, the revolutionaries aimed to reshape French society in accordance with their revolutionary ideals, laying the groundwork for a nation built on principles of reason and republicanism.

CHAPTER 4:

WHAT REPLACED PAPAL MONARCHY, THE ARISTOCRACY, SPIRITUAL OVERSIGHT OF THE CATHOLIC CHURCH, AND TRADITION?

Because the revolutionaries despised the Pope, Monarchy, the Catholic Church, the Aristocracy, and Tradition, they developed a new system based on this radical sense of egalitarianism that came from Enlightenment thinking, based on the ideas of Rousseau, Voltaire, Thomas Paine, John Locke, and others. Instead of a king ruling by Catholic spiritual oversight, you now had a secular state that was supreme over religion that fully implemented the meaning behind the social contract theory based on universal manhood suffrage and direct election by the people.[123] Instead of the king ruling, now there was a national legislature, and its officials were directly elected by the people. Along with the Declaration of the Rights of Man and Citizen, this new political system provided a radical sense of egalitarianism based on almost absolute human liberty, which basically meant doing anything a person wanted to do as long as it did not physically hurt others.

The new government saw to it that every citizen had the right to gain an education and subsistence. Because it made the Church subject to the new secular state, it took over the Church's once responsibilities and offered aid to the poor and even promised work to the unemployed.[124] The new secular state was based on giving almost absolute liberty to the people. It took over education from the Catholic Church and offered a public

---

[123] Desan, S., & Company, T. (2013). Living the French Revolution and the Age of Napoleon. The Great Courses, pg. 183
[124] Ibid

education to the people, called for free trade to cancel out the old guild system and aristocratic privilege, sought an idea of republicanism, and sought to better life for the people by being for things that constituted economic progress for the people.[125]

Even though what we would call conservatives today argued that voting power should only go to men who paid a large amount in taxes, universal manhood suffrage won out at the end of the day.[126] Since they sought to weaken and destroy the Catholic Church along with the belief that men should be able to believe in anything they wanted as long as it did not physically hurt others, they decided to extend rights to Protestants, who were considered heretics. Because the kingship got its legitimacy from the Catholic Church to rule, they decided to weaken the Church as much as possible because they now believed from the social contract theory that legitimacy and sovereignty did not come from the Church as they once did. It then claimed that sovereignty and legitimacy come from the nation as a whole.[127]

Instead of a king, aristocracy, and a powerful church wielding power, power now rested in the hands of citizens who vote; the voting public became quasi-divine in the new secular republic. They came up with the idea of freedom of thought, worship, and conscience and that rights should be extended to all. Here, protestants and Jews were given equal rights. Catholicism became just a religion like any other. In the old regime of France, the clergy pushed the king to make a "solemn declaration" that he would only allow Catholicism to reign in France and never allow the free exercise of any other religion in France because his job was to root out heresy to keep unity in religion, because of the Petrine doctrine; here the revolutionaries sought to eradicate the notion of religious unity.[128] They ensured that Catholics were now on the same footing with unbelievers and even protestants, and they made sure not a single cleric nor bishop was involved in

---

[125] Kennedy, Emmet. A Cultural History of the French Revolution. New Haven, Yale University Press, 1989, pg. 375
[126] Desan, S., & Company, T. (2013). Living the French Revolution and the Age of Napoleon. The Great Courses, pg. 81
[127] Ibid, pg. 65
[128] McManners, John. The French Revolution and the Church. Church Historical Society, 1969, pg. 6

political matters. This way, they ensured secular supremacy and could freely legislate in matters of marriage, family, education, etc.[129]

The Enlightenment and Revolution destroyed the classical world; they destroyed the concepts of divine monarchy, religion, tradition, and natural hierarchy of kings over their subjects, aristocrats over commoners, and fathers over their wives and children. These were all the state of normality before the revolution.[130] Ever since this time, there has always been a conservative movement that struggled against the Enlightenment and Revolution on how these things destroyed the classical world. The conservative movement argued that simply breaking with the past and producing a radically new system of government and rule brought chaos and uncertainty and that hierarchy and patriarchalism produced stability and orderliness in society.[131] They argued that the clergy regains its omnipresence in politics, education, and culture.[132] Yet liberalism emerged, which argued for civil liberties, constitutionalism, representative government, freedom of the press, speech, religion, etc.[133]

---

[129] Ibid, pg. 40, 141-143
[130] Desan, S., & Company, T. (2013). Living the French Revolution and the Age of Napoleon. The Great Courses, pg. 333
[131] Ibid
[132] Ibid
[133] Ibid, pg. 334

THE SELF-CROWNED EMPEROR: NAPOLEON'S SECULAR ASSERTION AGAINST THE CHURCH

Napoleon Bonaparte's rise to power as the successor of the French Revolution was a complex interplay of military prowess, political acumen, and popular appeal. The French Revolution, which began in 1789, dismantled the old regime, overthrowing the monarchy and establishing a republic. In the ensuing chaos, the revolutionary government oscillated between radical and moderate phases, ultimately leading to the rise of the Directory, a five-member committee that governed France from 1795. However, the Directory was rife with corruption and inefficiency, paving the way for a strong leader to emerge.

Napoleon, a brilliant military general, capitalized on his successes in the Italian campaigns and his popularity with the army and the public. In 1799, he orchestrated a coup d'état, known as the Coup of 18 Brumaire, effectively ending the Directory and establishing the Consulate, with himself as First Consul. By 1804, he had consolidated enough power to crown himself Emperor of the French, signaling both the end of the revolutionary period and the beginning of his imperial rule.

Napoleon's relationship with the Catholic Church was marked by pragmatic manipulation and strategic dominance. One of the most significant events in this context was the imprisonment of Pope Pius VII. This action stemmed from the wider conflict between Napoleon's secular ambitions and the Church's spiritual authority. Initially, Napoleon sought to reconcile with the Church through the Concordat of 1801, which reestablished the Catholic Church in France but on terms favorable to the state. However, as Napoleon's empire expanded, his demands on the Church grew more severe. The Pope's refusal to support Napoleon's Continental System, a blockade against British trade, led to escalating tensions. In 1809, Napoleon ordered the annexation of the papal states and the subsequent arrest and imprisonment of Pius VII. The Pope was held in captivity until 1814, symbolizing Napoleon's assertion of secular supremacy over the Church.

The act of crowning himself emperor was a definitive statement of Napoleon's secular authority. Traditionally, the crowning of a monarch by the Pope was a powerful symbol of divine sanction and spiritual legitimacy. Napoleon inverted this symbolism by taking the crown from Pope Pius VII's hands while he turned his back to the Pope and placing it on his head during the coronation ceremony in Notre Dame Cathedral in 1804[134]. He demonstrated that his authority was derived not from the Church but from his own achievements and the will of the people. This bold move underscored his belief in the primacy of secular power and the subordination of religious authority to the state. It also reinforced his image as a self-made ruler, a man who had risen from modest beginnings to the pinnacle of power through his own merits.

The significance of Napoleon crowning himself extended beyond a mere assertion of independence from the Church. It marked a new era in the relationship between the state and religion, one where the state asserted its dominance over spiritual matters. This act resonated throughout Europe, signaling a shift toward secularism that would influence political thought and statecraft in the centuries to follow. By positioning himself as the embodiment of both revolutionary ideals and imperial authority, Napoleon reshaped the political landscape of Europe and left a lasting legacy on the interplay between secular and spiritual power. His goal was the same as the French Revolution had implemented in regard to the Catholic Church. He made sure that the secular state was over the religion and that minority faith was to be recognized.[135]

---

[134] Desan, S., & Company, T. (2013). Living the French Revolution and the Age of Napoleon. The Great Courses, pg. 269
[135] Desan, S., & Company, T. (2013). Living the French Revolution and the Age of Napoleon. The Great Courses, pg. 304

CONCLUSION

In conclusion, the French Revolution brought about a profound transformation in the relationship between the Catholic Church and the state, marking a significant shift from the traditional balance of spiritual and temporal power. The Revolution effectively subordinated the Church to secular authority, disrupting the longstanding hierarchical order where the Church served as the moral compass and overseer of government actions. This dramatic change paved the way for the complete secularization of society, fundamentally altering the nature of governance and social order.

The philosophical underpinnings, legislative changes, and societal impacts that facilitated this shift are crucial for understanding these historical transformations. In pre-revolutionary France, divine providence governed both religious and secular affairs, with the Catholic Church and the Pope serving as earthly mediators of this divine order. The Church's influence reinforced the hierarchical structure of society, legitimizing the divine right of kings and ensuring social stability.

Furthermore, the aristocracy and clergy occupied privileged positions in society, exempt from taxation and benefiting from feudal dues, respectively. Marriage and family life were deeply rooted in religious and social frameworks governed by the Catholic Church through canon law. Patriarchy and primogeniture maintained the social and political order, concentrating authority in the hands of men and preserving noble lineages' power.

The peasantry formed the backbone of society, enduring heavy taxation and feudal obligations while sustaining the kingdom's economy. The Catholic Church's monopoly on religion regulated public and private life, ensuring social cohesion and moral order.

The French Revolution's impact on the relationship between the Catholic Church and the state was profound, ushering in an era of secularization and challenging the entrenched hierarchies of pre-revolutionary France. Understanding these changes is essential for comprehending the deep-rooted transformations in church-state dynamics and their broader implications for modern society.

The pre-revolutionary educational system in France was intricately intertwined with the Catholic Church, which wielded significant control over both its content and purpose. Education served dual roles: nurturing faithful Christians and preparing future leaders loyal to the monarchy. The curriculum, rooted in classical education and Catholic doctrine, reinforced the social and hierarchical order aligned with the Church's teachings. This system was a powerful tool for maintaining spiritual and temporal authority, ensuring a generation steeped in tradition and loyal to the established order.

The Enlightenment posed a significant challenge to the traditional structures upheld by the Church and monarchy. Deism and Theophilanthropy redefined religious belief, promoting rational spirituality and moralistic faith grounded in human reason. Enlightenment ideals emphasized reason, empirical evidence, and secular governance, challenging religious dogma and advocating for equality and individual rights. This intellectual rebellion laid the groundwork for the revolutionary changes that would follow, reshaping French society and influencing democratic movements worldwide.

Rousseau's Social Contract Theory and the Declaration of the Rights of Man and the Citizen epitomized these Enlightenment ideals, advocating for popular sovereignty, individual rights, and secular governance. These foundational documents challenged the old order, promoted secularism, and laid the ideological groundwork for modern democratic states.

The French Revolution extended beyond political and social realms to fundamentally alter the structure of the family.

Revolutionaries sought to dismantle the patriarchal and religiously controlled family structure, promoting individual autonomy and equality. Changes to inheritance laws aimed to disrupt the economic and social stability that upheld the noble class and monarchy, fostering a society based on egalitarian principles and individual rights.

In pre-revolutionary France, the Catholic Church wielded immense influence over spiritual, temporal, political, and economic spheres. Its symbiotic relationship with the monarchy and pervasive control over governance, education, and morality underscored its authority. However, the Enlightenment challenged the Church's dominance, advocating for reason, secular governance, and individual rights, ultimately reshaping French society and laying the groundwork for modern democratic principles.

The Catholic Church wielded immense power and influence across various spheres of pre-revolutionary France, shaping societal structures and maintaining the status quo. However, the French Revolution aimed to dismantle this dominance, challenging the Church's authority in religious, political, economic, and social realms. Revolutionaries targeted the Church's privileges, property, and hierarchical control, seeking to establish a secular state based on equality and individual liberty principles. By nationalizing Church property, abolishing the tithe, and promoting freedom of conscience, the revolutionaries undermined the Church's economic and social power, fundamentally reshaping the relationship between religion and state in France.

Napoleon Bonaparte's self-coronation as Emperor of the French represented a pivotal moment in the history of state-church relations. His rise to power, rooted in the revolutionary upheavals that dismantled the old regime, exemplified the transition from monarchical and religious authority to secular dominance. By crowning himself, Napoleon boldly asserted that his legitimacy derived from his own achievements and the will of the people, not from divine sanction. This act, coupled with his pragmatic manipulation of the Catholic Church and the imprisonment of Pope Pius VII, underscored his commitment to establishing the supremacy of the secular state over spiritual authority. Napoleon's policies and actions marked a significant shift toward secularism, influencing political thought and governance in Europe for generations. His legacy as a self-made ruler who prioritized state control over religious influence continues to resonate, highlighting the enduring impact of his reign on the balance between secular and spiritual power.

In summary, the French Revolution's nationalization of Church property and abolition of the tithe were pivotal steps in establishing a secular state and dismantling feudal structures. These actions relieved rural populations of burdens and symbolized a commitment to equality and church-state separation. The assault on monasticism furthered this agenda, eradicating traditional religious structures and paving the way for a secular society. The revolution's de-Christianization efforts, persecution of the clergy, and introduction of the Republican Calendar all contributed to reshaping French society along secular and rationalist lines. Rooted in Enlightenment ideals, the revolutionaries aimed to replace divine monarchy and religious authority with a secular, democratic system founded on equality and liberty, marking a profound departure from the past and laying the groundwork for modern democratic societies.

BIBLIOGRAPHY

Desan, S., & Company, T. (2013). Living the French Revolution and the Age of Napoleon. The Great Courses

Doyle, W. (2018). The Oxford History of the French Revolution. Oxford University Press.

Huntington, S. P. (1993). The clash of civilizations? Foreign Affairs, 72(3), 25

Internet History Sourcebooks Project. Sourcebooks.fordham.edu, sourcebooks.fordham.edu/source/B8-unam.asp.

Kennedy, Emmet. A Cultural History of the French Revolution. New Haven, Yale University Press, 1989.

McManners, John. The French Revolution and the Church. Church Historical Society, 1969.